The Falklands Regime

By

Mike Bingham

authorHOUSE™

1663 LIBERTY DRIVE, SUITE 200
BLOOMINGTON, INDIANA 47403
(800) 839-8640
WWW.AUTHORHOUSE.COM

First published by AuthorHouse 05/27/05

ISBN: 1-4208-1375-7 (sc)

Printed in the United States of America
Bloomington, Indiana

This book is printed on acid-free paper.

Cover photo: Falklands beach covered in dead penguins, May 2002.

PART 1: The road to conflict

"Life is what you make it...
....if fate permits it."

CHAPTER ONE

October 1974. I was a typical student studying A' levels, not because I had any clear idea of where I was heading in life, but simply because I had followed the well rutted path of education, without really questioning if it was the right direction for me. Relatives, teachers and friends all urged me to study hard and go to university, and why not, it seemed better than getting a job, but it was no mean feat for somebody with no aptitude for study. I much preferred to spend my evenings playing with my motorcycles, and riding for miles in order to feel the cool evening breeze in my face, and the sense of freedom in my soul. It was on just such an evening that a chance meeting was to change my life forever.

The autumn evening air was still warm, and the dying sun cast its golden fingers across the distant city. I had been riding for over an hour, and was now heading back towards Manchester's city centre. Such rides usually helped me clear my mind of the stresses of city life, but tonight I had been constantly nagged by the knowledge that I had not really spent enough time on the biology assignment that I had completed some two hours previously. In reality there was little point in worrying about it, since I had no intention of spending further time on it, and it was due in the following day in any case.

I turned off the motorway and headed towards a quiet pub, which I sometimes visited for a cool beer before returning home. Even though I was only sixteen years old, I never had trouble getting served at this particular pub. My motorcycle helped. In reality it was only a 50cc moped, but it had gears, did 50mph, and looked every bit like a real motorcycle.

As I neared the final bend, a roar of thunder and a flash of green shot past me. I swerved towards the curb, narrowly missing a huge American car shooting past, hotly pursued by a bright red Mini. I missed the curve by a whisker and regained control of the bike. Shakily I reached the club and turned into the car park, where the first sights to greet me were the green Pontiac and red Mini. I parked the bike beside the two cars and strode round to confront the occupiers. As I removed my helmet, a pretty young girl with straight blond hair stepped from the Mini.

"Are you okay?" She asked, with what seemed like genuine concern.

"No thanks to your driving." I replied dryly, my anger somewhat frustrated by being faced with such a pretty young lady.

"Hey look, I'm sorry. But I didn't cut you in, did I? I was just trying to follow him." She pointed to the bearded man stepping from the Pontiac.

"Is he starting trouble?" The man shouted across to her.

"No, no!" She insisted anxiously. "I was just making sure he was okay."

"If he can't take care of himself on the road, he shouldn't have left his mother's tit." The man sneered through his thick, black beard.

"I think you need driving lessons." I told him bluntly.

"I think you're looking for a slapping," the man said stepping forward, "and you're going to get it if you don't piss off."

"No, please don`t start...." The girl begged, but to no avail as he proceeded to step forward and take a big swing at me.

I was startled by the sudden attack, not to mention his size. I would have backed off but for the fact that I did not want to look a coward in front of the girl. Even though the man was large, he was incredibly slow, and by grabbing his arm I was able to turn him around and throw him onto the ground. The girl laughed. I was astonished at myself, and more than a little thrilled, until the man got back onto his feet again.

This time he looked really angry, and began to think I should run, but he came at me again before I had time to decide. As he lunged at me I turned side on and kicked him in the stomach. I moved back more than he did, but it left him doubled over clutching his belly in pain. With my adrenaline now flowing, and not wanting to give him another chance to recover, I hit him on the side of his head, and he fell spread-eagled on the ground. This time he did not get up. The girl looked down at him in disgust.

"I didn't mean to hurt your friend." I apologised, beginning to feel guilty at letting my temper run away in such a fashion.

"Don`t apologise." She bent down to take a look at the groaning figure on the ground. "He's no friend of mine, and he's had that coming for a long time. I think he's okay."

The man rolled over and put his hand to the side of his head, swearing and cursing under his breath. The girl helped him to sit up, and I watched her as she did so. She was extremely pretty, about five foot eight inches tall, slim in build, and in her early twenties. Her platinum blonde hair was straight, and cut to just above shoulder length. Her lips curled up into a half smile as she helped the man to his feet, trying not to laugh at his misfortune.

Once he was back on his feet, the man pushed her away angrily, and staggered off into the club.

"My name's Mike." I introduced myself.

"Hi, I'm Jackie." The girl replied. "And the arsehole was Ken. Sorry he couldn't hang around for a proper introduction. I'm ashamed to say he used to be my boyfriend until a week ago. He cut a young lad up badly last week when he was out with his mates, and doesn't care at all. Its about time he got a taste of his own medicine."

"Have you known him long?" I asked, looking for something to say rather than out of genuine curiosity.

"No. About four weeks. Long enough I reckon." As she spoke, the door burst open, and Ken came out with two mates.

"If you start trouble now you'll be sorry." Jackie shouted at Ken, with a hint of panic in her voice.

"You think I'm just going to let it drop, do you?" Ken shouted, pointing at me. "Nobody hits me when my back is turned and gets away with it."

"What are you going to prove with three of you?" Jackie asked. "Does that make you a man?"

"You keep out of this." Ken pointed at Jackie angrily. "I don't mind hitting a woman if I have to"

"Oh I don't doubt that for a minute." Jackie sneered. "But think on this. If you hurt him now, I'm going to the police with everything I know, and that includes last week's incident. You got that."

"Don't you threaten me, you bitch." Ken stepped towards her with his fists raised.

"Leave her. It's me you want." I tried to sound relaxed, but my heart was pounding, and my voice betrayed my fear.

Jackie held out her palm to shut me up. "It's okay, Mike. Ken might be a thug, but he's not stupid enough to risk prison for this. Are you dear?." She stared straight at him coldly.

Ken could see that Jackie meant every word. His friends looked to him for guidance, but he said nothing.

Jackie held out her hand to me. "Come on Mike, it's time to go."

I did not stop to ask where. I followed her slowly towards the vehicles, keeping a careful eye on Ken as he stood wondering what to do. I pulled on my helmet, and without waiting to fasten it, started up the bike and rode out of the carpark behind Jackie's Mini.

I had no idea where she was going, but I was determined to follow her. If I lost sight of her I had no idea who she was, or where I could find her again. I didn't even know if she really wanted me to follow her or not. All I knew for sure was that I was going to follow her until she stopped, wherever that might lead.

We joined the motorway and followed it for several miles. I wasn't supposed to be on a motorway with a provisional license, but I had no intention of stopping. Eventually Jackie turned off and drove into the carpark of a small country pub, and I parked up beside her.

"Are you coming in?" She gestured to the door.

"Yes, sure." I nodded.

Jackie made her way over to an empty table in the far corner, while I went to the bar to buy drinks. The barmaid gave me a disapproving look, and my heart sank as I realised she was going to ask my age. How would I live it down if I was refused drinks in front of Jackie?

The barmaid looked across to the table where Jackie sat combing her hair, and then back to me. "Yes dear." She smiled. "What would you like?"

I ordered a gin and tonic for Jackie, and a beer for myself, and took them across to where Jackie was sitting.

"Are you okay?" Jackie asked me.

"Yes, sure. No problem." I said, trying to exude an air of confidence. "Why do you ask?"

"Oh, no reason really." She looked at me with tender, sensitive blue eyes, that seemed to probe my very soul. I felt uncomfortable and looked away.

"I expect Ken had a shock tonight." I said, for the want of something to say to break the silence.

"It's about time that he had more than a shock." Jackie showed no sympathy. "He really is a nasty piece of work. I don't know what I ever saw in him. He is so rude, he's had more than one slap across his face from me in public, I can tell you, and each time he just passes it off as a joke to his friends. But don't be fooled, even his friends would stab him in the back given a good enough reason. They're all the same, I've never met such an odd bunch."

"Did you go there with him tonight?" I was confused.

"You must be joking!" Jackie wrinkled up her nose, and took another sip of her gin and tonic. "He's like a big kid. He overtook me on a blind bend, presumably to show off after I dumped him last week, so I stuck to his tail all the way to the club. That must have got right up his nose. What with him having a big, powerful Pontiac, and being unable to outpace my little Mini. That's probably why he got out of the car in such a bad mood."

"Yes, that might explain it." I said sarcastically, taking another sip of beer. "So you don't see him any more?"

"No." Jackie smiled. I smiled back nervously. I was captivated by her inviting blue eyes, that made her look so sweet and innocent. I thought she was the prettiest girl I had ever seen, and as we talked, I felt myself being drawn closer and closer towards her.

I asked her about her family.

7

"I have no brothers or sisters." She explained, with a hint of regret in her voice. "I don`t really get on all that well with my parents either. I'm a disappointment to them. They think I'm common because I work as a barmaid."

"I don`t see anything wrong with working as a barmaid" I assured her. "They should be proud to have a daughter like you."

"They don`t seem to think so." She looked down at her drink thoughtfully. "They never had very much time for me, even as a child. It was only my uncle that ever showed any real interest in me. I still live with my parents, but I want to get a flat of my own just as soon as I can afford one. Maybe they will respect me more when I can stand on my own feet."

"Perhaps they do respect you, but find it hard to show it."

"I don`t think so." Jackie shook her head. "If only they could treat me like my uncle used to. We used to understand each other. He thought the world of me and used to take me places when I was a child, and gave me the chance to do the things other children used to do. We used to have a lot of fun together. Neither of us really had anybody else. He never married, and had no other family apart from my father, who was his brother. I think that's why we were so close."

"Why do you keep referring to him in the past tense?"

"He died last year."

"Oh. I'm sorry." I took hold of her hand and squeezed it gently.

Jackie looked up at me and smiled briefly. "I used to go to his house every weekend. My parents were glad to be free of me. He was a lovely man, always smiling and joking. He told me that a girl on her own was in constant danger in a city like this, and that I should always be on my guard. He was very worried that harm might come to me when I'm alone."

"There's sense in that I suppose, especially for a woman." I suddenly became conscious of the fact that I was staring at her, and looked down at my drink. "Where do you live?"

"In Salford."

"Is that where you work, too?"

"Yes not far away, near the city centre. That's where I met that creep, Ken." She shook her head casually. "What do you do?"

I paused for a moment, wondering what to say. "I'm a student." I said reluctantly.

"You must be clever." Jackie said it half jokingly, but her eyes showed that she was not mocking. "I left school at sixteen. I never had any interest in school work. I was in too much of a rush to see the real world, and having seen it I can tell you you're better off where you are."

"So everyone keeps telling me." I was not convinced. "How come you're not behind the bar tonight?" I enquired, trying to change the subject.

"I only work four nights a week, and three afternoons. It's funny hours, but the pay's not too bad."

"Are you off tomorrow night?" I felt a hot wave come over me as I asked the question. It was clear that she was in her early twenties, and it hardly seemed likely that she would be interested in someone who was barely turned sixteen.

"No, not until the night after. Do you want to meet up somewhere then?"

"Em, yes sure." I was slightly surprised by the directness of her reply.

"Okay. Why don`t you meet me here about seven, and we can go on somewhere afterwards. Do you like dancing?"

"Yes, to the right music." I could hardly control my excitement. "Do you know of any good places?"

"There is a place I used to visit every week, which I haven't been to for months. Do you fancy giving that a try?"

"That sounds great." I agreed with as much self-control as my dancing heart would allow.

Jackie finished her drink. "Well, I`d better be moving." She got up, and stroked my cheek gently with the palm of her hand. "I'll see you."

I wanted to stand up and kiss her, but my legs refused to obeyed, and then she was gone.

I leaned back in my chair, and let out a deep sigh. Taking a sip of my beer, I thought back over the extraordinary events of the evening. It all seemed like a fantasy. I had never really believed in love at first sight, but my feelings for this girl had sent me into turmoil. I knew that I would count every second until I saw her again. I had always been very independent, and yet now I felt empty without her. Like a football stadium after the players and spectators had all gone home. Forty four hours seemed like an eternity; would they ever pass?

I finished my drink, and went out into the carpark. The air was cold, and the moon shone like a giant eye watching over me. Looking up at the stars, I thought how small and insignificant I was in the vastness of the universe. Yet somehow I felt very important tonight, more important than I had ever felt. It seemed as though for the first time in my life, I actually knew where I was heading.

I looked across to my bike, and brought myself back to reality. How could my life possibly have taken on such a new purpose? I had only met her a couple of hours before. If I faced the truth the chances were that she'd never show. Perhaps not, but one thing was for sure, I would be there to find out.

CHAPTER TWO

The two days passed ever so slowly, but eventually they did pass, and by a quarter to seven in the evening I was sat in the pub waiting for Jackie to arrive. I chewed my nails nervously, pausing only to look at the clock as it edged its way towards seven o'clock. My stomach felt as though it had knots tied in it, and I had eaten virtually nothing since breakfast. My gut feeling told me that she would show, but I could not quell a nagging doubt that I was kidding myself. Maybe on reflection she would think that I was too young for her. If truth be told, I probably was.

The door opened. My eyes fixed on the doorway: it was a man who entered. I sighed and looked at the clock again, before returning to the task of chewing my nails. Maybe she had met somebody else? My mind explored every possible reason for her failing to show, whilst my eyes kept glancing from the door to the clock, and back to the door again. It was now five past seven, and still no sign. Now I really did begin to worry. How could I find her if she didn't show? I began to wonder whether she had given me enough information for me to be able to find the pub where she worked. If only I had asked the name of the pub.

The door opened again, and in breezed the tall, slim, platinum blonde who had captured my heart. Her hair shone like strands of pure gold in the coloured lighting of the bar. Her white blouse, and black ankle length maxi skirt, followed every curve of her shapely body.

I leapt to my feet with boyish exuberance, and offered her a drink.

"I'd like a gin and tonic, please." She asked, obviously sensing how anxious I was. "I'm so glad you waited for me. I'm sorry to be late for our first date. My Mini started overheating again, and I had to stop at the garage for water."

"Hey, that's okay. Don't worry about it." My ego lifted. "I'm just glad you decided to show." I picked up the drinks from the bar, and handed Jackie her gin and tonic.

"Of course I did: why wouldn't I?" She took the drink, and we looked around to find a table. The pub was quiet, with just three people sat at one of the tables, and a man stood on his own at the end of the bar.

The pub was small and cosy, with nine antique style oak tables, each surrounded by stools upholstered in burgundy crushed velvet. The room was bathed in soft orange light from three chandeliers, and the beam ceilings and antique brasses gave the pub a sense of warmth and splendour.

"What time does the dance start?" I enquired, feeling slightly more at ease.

"About eight o'clock." Jackie glanced at her watch. "Do you want to leave your bike here, and come in the car with me?"

"Yes, sure." I smiled and glanced down at her long, tight-fitting dress. "You're not really dressed to come on the bike, are you?"

"I guess not. Do you trust women drivers?"

"I trust you." I said softly. Jackie looked up at me invitingly, and I seized the opportunity to take hold of her hand. She squeezed my hand tightly, and smiled affectionately. I felt a tingle running through my entire body. Every problem I had ever had was wiped away in an instant: nothing but the present mattered.

"You say that now," Jackie teased me, "but you haven't been in the car with me yet."

"I'm sure your driving can't be that bad. Can it?"

Jackie shrugged and smiled. "You'll have to wait and see."

"Like I said, I trust you. How far is it anyway?"

"Not far, but we better leave soon." Jackie glanced at her watch again. "We don`t want to be too late arriving. They only let so many people in."

I swigged down the remainder of my beer. "Ready when you are."

Jackie finished her drink and we left. The night air was getting cold. Winter was drawing closer it seemed, but at least it was not raining. Not that we would have noticed if it had been, we were both too busy enjoying each others company to notice trivialities such as the weather.

Jackie's car stood in the car park next to my motorcycle. I threw my helmet onto the back seat as we climbed in, and looked across at Jackie. Our eyes met. Nervously I put my arm around her shoulders, and she moved across to me, taking hold of my hand. Her sparkling blue eyes beckoned. I stroked her silk like hair and kissed her gently on the lips. She placed her arms around me and hugged me tightly, pressing her lips tightly against mine. I felt a tingle ripple through my body as I melted into her arms. Her love and affection surrounded me like a mysterious and precious cocoon, insulating me from the outside world. All I could feel was her silky wet lips against mine, her warm breath against my cheek, and her curvaceous body held tightly against me by our embrace.

"I'm so glad I met you." I said, for the need of something to say.

"So am I." Jackie replied softly, squeezing me tightly.

Both of us became so engrossed in each others company, talking, kissing, and lying in each others arms, that we failed to notice how time was passing, until Jackie noticed the clock in the dashboard.

"Hey, look at the time." She said, wriggling back into the driver's seat. "We better get a move on or we won't get in."

She started up the car and screeched around the car park towards the exit. There was nothing coming, so she shot out into the road, and tore off down the road. I felt myself being pushed back into the seat by the acceleration. This was no ordinary Mini. I looked across to Jackie with a somewhat startled expression.

"Are you okay?" Jackie asked calmly. The speedometer was showing nearly sixty miles per hour, with a sharp bend looming ever closer, and we were still accelerating!

"Yes, yes, I'm fine" I replied, fumbling for the seat belt. "I like fast driving."

My eyes were fixated on the road ahead. I had never been so terrified in a car in all my life. No matter how hard I tried to distract my thoughts, I couldn't help returning to the question of whether the car would actually stay on the road around the next bend. I certainly wasn't going to let Jackie know how nervous I felt though, so I tried to remain as calm as my circumstances would allow, and prayed that we didn't have too far to go.

"We're about half way there." Jackie informed me, as the car raced towards a humpback bridge. As the car shot over the bridge, the wheels momentarily left the ground. Immediately beyond the bridge lay a sharp left-hand bend, and we touched down just in time to make the turn, I let out a huge sigh of relief. Then I saw what lay ahead. At the worst possible moment on this blind bend, the road was completely blocked by a tractor reversing a trailer into a gateway. There was nowhere to go.

I felt myself being thrown forward, stopped only by the seat belt, but the expected bang never came. I looked up, and to my amazement, not to say relief, we had come to a complete stop. The tractor, which was still several yards in front of us, continued backing in. I looked across to Jackie.

"What a silly place to have a gateway." She remarked casually.

"Quite." I replied, unable to think of anything else to say.

The tractor completed its turn, and we accelerated off down the road once more. Completely numbed by our near collision with the tractor, I lay back quietly for the remainder of the journey.

The club car park was full when we arrived, but we managed to get into a space vacated by somebody just leaving.

"I hope we can still get in." I said, taking hold of Jackie's hand as we walked across the car park.

"It looks as though we're in luck," Jackie pointed to the entrance, "people are still going in."

We joined the small queue of people waiting at the door, and after a short wait we were admitted. I bought the tickets, and followed Jackie through to the dance floor. It was an enormous hall, with tables and chairs around the perimeter, a large bar at the far end, and a huge dance floor in the centre. There must have been two to three hundred people inside the hall, and there were still tables free.

Jackie took possession of a table while I fetched some drinks. The queue at the bar was about three deep along its entire length, but with eleven bar staff serving, it did not take too long to get served. I paid for the drinks and began to look around for where Jackie had gone. I had not really taken much notice of which table she had taken, an oversight which I now regretted. With so many tables around the room, it became obvious that it could take some time to find her, and I decided to return to where we had parted and begin my search from there. As I neared the entrance, I spotted her waving to me, and made my way over.

"It would be easy to get lost in here." I remarked casually as I placed the drinks on the table.

"Wait till later when people are on the dance floor, you'd never find anybody then." Jackie took a sip of her drink. "That's why I was in a rush to get here. I hope I didn't scare you too much."

"A bit perhaps," I admitted, "but I got used to it. You seemed to know what you were doing"

"Don't worry, I don't usually drive like that." Jackie laughed, but I didn't feel that she was laughing at me. She took hold of my hand which I had resting on the table, and entwined her fingers with mine.

"I don't mind. Like I said, I trust you." I stroked her hand softly and looked deeply into her sparkling blue eyes. I felt much more at ease with her now. She moved closer to me, and I put my arms around her and kissed her.

As we kissed, the lights dimmed, and the music which had been gently in the background suddenly punched its way into life through eight massive speakers dotted around the hall. The whole dance floor was illuminated by a spectrum of pulsating lights. The disco was underway, and people began making their way up to dance.

"Do you want to dance?" Jackie shouted, standing up but still holding my hand.

"Do I have to?" I asked half jokingly.

"Yes." Jackie pulled my arm with such a force, that I toppled from my chair and landed on the floor. Jackie burst out laughing. Composing herself once more, she offered me her hand to help me up, but instead of using it to pull myself up, I yanked her arm down, and she landed on the floor beside me. We both sat on the floor in a heap, laughing until our sides were aching.

"I'm sure people think we're mad." I whispered in her ear. People on the surrounding tables were watching us with a mixture of amusement and disapproval. Jackie glanced around at the people watching, then back to me, and burst out laughing once more. I helped her to her feet, and dragged her by the hand onto the dance floor, where we began to dance.

The atmosphere was electric. Within minutes of starting, the enormous dance floor was vibrant and alive. Jackie and I remained on the dance floor for most of the evening; right through to the slow romantic music, and I was able to take Jackie in my arms once more. She rested her head on my shoulder, as we moved together to the slow beat of the music. She was exhausted, and with my hand around her, I could feel her blouse sticking to her back from perspiration. I was awash with a warm inner glow of tranquillity.

When the music finally ended, and the main lights came on, we wandered slowly back to our table and flopped down onto the chairs. Jackie finished off the last bit of her Gin and Tonic, and lent back in the chair. Her face was flushed, and her usually immaculate hair stuck to her forehead and neck. She brushed it back with her hand, and let out a deep sigh.

"You look how I feel." I teased her.

"Oh, I'm shattered." She gasped. "It always gets so hot in here."

As people began to leave, the fire exits around the hall, which had been kept closed all night, were now opened for people to leave by, creating a cooling breeze which felt refreshing.

"Do you think you can summon enough energy to make it as far as the car?" I teased her.

"I suppose I might, if I were to make a supreme effort. I might need a hand though." She held out her hand to me. I stood up and pulled her up from the chair. The autumn breeze had a cold bite to it, and was in sharp contrast to the hot, humid dance hall. We hurried across the large carpark under the bright romantic moonlight, and hopped into the car. Jackie sat sideways across both seats so that she was leaning back against me, and I placed my arms around her slender waist.

"What did you think of the place?" She took hold of one of my hands, and entwined her fingers with mine, palm to palm.

"I thought it was great. I really enjoyed myself."

"Good, so did I. I always like dancing." She put my hand to her mouth, and kissed it gently. "Mind you, this dress is not very suitable for dancing, but that's the fashion."

"I think it looks absolutely stunning. Well, that's to say you make it look absolutely stunning." I ran my finger delicately along her moist lips, delighting in the soft silky sensation that I felt. She opened her mouth slightly, and I responded by running my finger along the top of her teeth, and then deeper until I felt the soft, wet feel of her tongue. She closed her teeth on my finger gently, and sucked on it, whilst she caressed it slowly with her tongue. I would never have thought that such an experience could be so sensual. I brought my other hand up, and ran my fingers up the base of her neck and through her hair, sending goose-bumps down her spine.

"I'm glad you like my dress." She said as I removed my finger from her mouth. She put her hand behind my head and pulled me towards her waiting lips. Her kiss was warm and inviting, and as our teeth momentarily touched, I felt an electrical sensation run through me.

For over an hour we sat kissing, and making small talk, before finally tearing ourselves apart to drive back. This time she drove back at a slightly more leisurely pace, although by no stretch of the imagination could it have been said that she crawled back.

"Don`t you ever get stopped for speeding?" I asked for amazement.

"No. I never have been so far. I've just been lucky I guess."

"I`d say so." I shook my head and grinned.

"Not nervous are you?" She asked with concern.

"No, no, really I'm fine. It's just that if I rode my bike around at this speed I would be stopped by the police for sure. Not that my bike would actually do this speed"

"Motorbikes always attract a lot of attention from the police. Nobody pays much attention to an ordinary car like this though, unless you do something silly. It would be different if I jazzed it up with fancy wheels, a loud exhaust, and go-faster stripes, but who wants all that?" Jackie shrugged.

"Yes, quite."

We swung into the pub carpark where I had left my bike, and parked next to it.

"Are you free tomorrow night?" I asked confidently.

"No, I'm afraid not." She answered. " I won't be free until Sunday. Shall we go somewhere then?"

"Yes okay. I could meet you in the morning, and we could make a day of it if you like."

"Great. Do you want me to pick you up from your place?" Jackie asked.

"Em, yes okay." I hesitated. "I'll wait for you outside the Davyhulme Road newsagents if you like, do you know where that is?"

My parents were reasonably liberal, but I did not think that they were quite ready for my being picked up by a girl some 6 years my senior. I already received enough lectures about schoolwork commitment, or rather the lack of it. I didn't need any lectures about my social life as well, especially now that I actually had a social life.

"Sure. Eleven o'clock okay?" Jackie's eyes shone like jewels.

"Yes. I'll see you then." I put my arm around her and gave her one last lingering kiss. It was all I could do to tear myself away. I collected my helmet, and got out of the car. Jackie blew me a kiss, and left. As I watched her driving away down the road, an eerie sense of emptiness came over me once more. It would be another long wait before I would see her again, but this time things were very different. This time I knew that she would show.

CHAPTER THREE

It was five minutes to eleven, and I was standing at the junction by the shops where I had arranged to meet Jackie. A bright yellow Ford Capri caught my eye as it screeched to a halt across the road, but I continued to scan the road for Jackie's Mini.

"Hey, its me." Jackie shouted from the half open window of the Capri. I ran across and jumped in.

"I didn't recognise you in this." I explained, grinning at the excitement of seeing her again. "I couldn't see you through the tinted windows"

"Do you like it?" She asked excitedly. "I only got it yesterday."

"Yes, it's great." I looked around at the sumptuous black interior and the impressive row of dashboard instruments. It was a very stylish car. "What happened to the Mini?"

"I part exchanged it for this." Jackie put it into gear and accelerated away. I was pushed back into the seat fiercely as the car rocketed off down the road, to the accompaniment of squealing tyres. The speedometer shot up to 60 mph in seconds without even changing gear.

"What the hell is this?" I asked with astonishment.

"Its an RS3100." She said with a huge grin across her face. "I just couldn't resist it."

"I can see why." I drooled. "It's a dream car."

"What shall we do today?" Jackie asked, as we slowed down to a more sensible speed. "Go for a drive?"

"Sounds good to me. If you're hungry, I know a really nice place a few miles from here that serves great food. I've been there with my parents a few times"

"Okay, let's go."

We had lunch together at a rustic country inn near Lymm, and spent the rest of the day driving around from place to place, sight seeing, chatting, and getting to know each other. By evening we had reached a quiet hotel which Jackie knew of. I was certainly getting an education on Manchester's night-spots.

The hotel was divided up into several different rooms: the restaurant, a snooker room, the public bar where they had a jukebox, and the lounge bar. We were both feeling hungry again, and decided to go into the lounge bar to get bar meals.

The lounge bar was lavishly furnished, with thickly upholstered settees and chairs, and knee-high copper and oak tables. We sat down at the bar and took a look at the menu.

"I'll get these, this time." Jackie insisted.

We both ordered scampi and chips, and bought some drinks which we took over to the table by the window.

"Are you working tomorrow?" I asked her.

"Yes. My hours usually stay the same, so that I'm off on Sunday, Wednesday and Friday evenings. I also work three afternoons. I'd like to try and change it so that I work three evenings and four afternoons."

"I'm all for that." I agreed. "I'd get to see more of you."

"There's nothing to stop you coming along when I'm working, I suppose, but you might get pretty bored. I'm usually rushed off my feet in the evenings, so we'd hardly get a chance to talk. I expect you have studying to do anyway."

She wasn't wrong there. Even by my standards, my work had slipped during the last week.

"Yes, I do have a lot of work to do during weekdays. Mind you, I wouldn't say I do a lot of studying. I never seem to be able to get down to it. I have so many distractions."

"Like me you mean."

"You're the kind of distraction I need." I gazed deeply into her beckoning eyes. She looked stunning with her black trouser suit, gold chain belt, and straight blonde hair.

"Tell me something." She asked, adopting a look of curiosity. "Have you told your parents about me?"

"No, actually I haven't." I admitted. "Why do you ask?"

"I didn't think you had. That explains why you asked me to meet you by the shops. I thought it rather strange. Is it because I'm older than you?"

"Well, partly I suppose, but I'm not bothered by that. Don't think that." I felt embarrassed that she might

24

think I was hiding her from my family. I took hold of her hand and held it tightly between mine. "I don't really talk about romantic stuff with my parents. They already think I spend too much time enjoying myself, and not enough time studying as it is. They're probably right, but in your case you're more important to me than anything else, and they would never understand that. It's not worth the hassle of trying to explain."

Jackie lent over and kissed me gently on the cheek. "How well do you get on with them?" She asked.

"Very well. I've had a very happy childhood, and my parents are very understanding about most things. It's just that they do keep going on about revising. I can see their point, it's just that I have a different perspective of what is important in my life. I have done fine with my school exams, got lots of GCSEs and so forth, but I'm not sure that University is really what I want. Sometimes I feel I should give up my studies, and get a job."

"I wouldn't be in too much of a hurry to do that." Jackie shook her head, and took another sip of her drink. "If you've got the brains, you should make the most of them. It's hard to get a decent job without qualifications. What do you want to do eventually."

I shrugged my shoulders. "That's the problem, I don't have any definite ambitions. I'm keen on Biology, but I don't know what kind of job I want to do at the end of it."

The food which we had ordered arrived, neatly laid out in little wicker baskets lined with a serviette, and accompanied by a bowl of tartar sauce. The food was delicious, and we both ate in virtual silence, enjoying every last mouthful.

"That was superb." I used the serviette to wipe my mouth, before screwing it up and putting it in the basket with the cutlery.

"Yes it was. I've never actually eaten here before, but its definitely worth coming back." Jackie washed down the food with the last of her drink. "Do you want another drink?" She asked.

"Its my round." I insisted.

"No, I told you I'd pay tonight." Jackie took the glasses. "I earn good wages, I don't want you to pay for everything. I tell you what though, could you get me some cigarettes from the machine out in the hall, while I'm at the bar?" She started to look for change for the cigarette machine.

"It's okay, I've got change." I was surprised at the request for cigarettes though. "I didn't know that you smoke."

"I don't, they're for my mum. I promised to get her some while I was out. She prefers Benson and Hedges, but otherwise get anything."

I went through to the cigarette machine in the hall, but soon discovered that I did not have the correct change after all. I had been so determined not to let Jackie give me money for the cigarettes, that I had not considered whether I actually had the correct change. I had no intention of making a complete fool of myself by going back, so instead I went through to the public bar to ask for change. It was packed with people, and after a long wait at the bar, I got the change I needed, and made my way back to the cigarette machine.

I placed the coins in the slot, and selected the Benson and Hedges. Suddenly my head was sent spinning by a forceful blow to the back of my head, and I fell to the floor in a semi-consciousness state. I tried to lift myself onto my knees, but my head was spinning round and round. My strength drained from my body, and I fell face down on the floor. I became aware of a tremendous pain at the back of my head, and tried to focus my mind around what was happening to me.

"I thought it was you." I heard a voice that I half recognised, taunting me from behind.

I rolled over slightly onto my side, and saw smashed glass from a bottle lying beside me, amidst smears of blood. I turned my head to look up, and saw Jackie's old friend, Ken, standing over me with two of his mates.

"Didn't you see us in the bar? You should have come over for a chat." Ken smirked.

I tried to gather my strength in a supreme effort to get up, but I was still too dazed. Ken kicked me hard in the stomach, causing me to double up.

"Where do you think you're going?" Ken asked coldly. "I'm not finished with you yet."

"Come on Ken." One of his friends tugged on Ken's sleeve. "Let's go before someone comes. He's learnt his lesson, we don`t want to kill him?"

"Don`t we?" Ken stared back at his friend, with eyes that showed he had lost all sense of reason. He kicked me again, at which point Ken's friends decided they had had enough, and ran out. Ken gave me one last kick, and followed them out into the car park.

I tried again to get up, and finally managed to lift myself onto my hands and knees. I proceeded to crawl out through the doorway leading to the car park, and saw Ken and his mates laughing and clowning around as they headed towards their car. I could feel the blood running down around my neck, and dripping from my chin. I gritted my teeth, and dragged myself to my feet using the door frame for support.

Jackie was sitting at the table by the window, wondering why I was taking so long to get cigarettes. As she took another sip of her cola, she caught sight of Ken and his pals getting into the Pontiac, and knew immediately that something was wrong. She ran out into the hall, and stopped in her tracks as she saw the blood and smashed glass on the floor. She put her hand to her mouth, as a cold chill ran through her body.

By now Ken's car was driving around towards the exit. I had begun staggering towards them, and managed to pick up half a brick that was lying by the low wall of the carpark.

"No, Mike, stop." Jackie screamed as she ran out into the carpark, but her warning came too late.

As the car approached towards me on its way out of the carpark, I hurled the brick, hitting the car windscreen and shattering it. I dropped back down onto my hands and knees from the exertion. Even in my severely dazed state, I felt the satisfaction of hitting Ken's precious car.

The car screeched to a halt, and Ken got out in an absolute rage, and began heading towards me.

"Leave him alone you bastard." Jackie screamed as she ran over towards us. Ken saw her coming and stopped in his tracks.

"Leave it. It's not worth it." A voice shouted to him from the car. "Let's get out of here."

Ken reluctantly got back in the car, and drove off, breaking the remainder of the windscreen away so that he could see to drive.

"Mike." Jackie threw herself to the floor, and put her arms round me to lift me into a sitting position. "Are you hurt bad? What did they do to you?"

"I'm okay I think. Just a bit groggy." I put my arm around her for support, and saw tears rolling down her cheeks. I put my hand up to wipe away the tears, and ended up smearing blood across her cheek instead. Her water filled eyes were huge with fear, as she looked at the blood streaked across my face and neck. She took a handkerchief from her pocket, and pressed it onto the wound to stop the bleeding.

"He took me by surprise from behind, I didn't even know he was there till he hit me with the bottle." I tried to explain; my speech slightly slurred.

"Shhhh. Don't try to talk." She held me tightly, feeling the warm sticky blood against her cheek. "You've lost a lot of blood, we need to get you to a doctor."

"There's no need for that, it looks worse than it is." I assured her. "Head wounds always bleed a lot, but it'll stop soon."

"What am I supposed to do with you." Jackie wept.

"Help me to my feet." I put my arm around her shoulders, and with her holding me around my waist, I managed to scramble to my feet.

"There that's better." I tried to sound encouraging, but my slurred speech just made Jackie feel more anxious.

"Please let me take you to a hospital."

"I'll be okay. If we go to the hospital, we'll have to explain to the police what happened. We really don't want to go through all that, do we." I looked at her, waiting for her to agree.

"Look, it won't take us long to get to my house. I'll take you there and clean you up, but if you don't look any better when I get you there, I'm calling the doctor" Jackie was determined.

I agreed, and we made our way towards the car. Jackie returned to the bar to fetch her purse, which held the car keys. Remarkably it was still there, and she drove me to her house.

"If my mother's in a bad mood, just ignore her." Jackie warned me as we pulled up outside. "She doesn't like me bringing boyfriends home, at the best of times."

The house was a typical Manchester-style three bedroom terraced house, but the inside was beautifully furnished, with thick carpets, and a delightful mixture of antique and modern furniture. Jackie led me through to the kitchen, and sat me down by the table where she prepared a bowl of hot water and antiseptic.

"Are you sure you're okay?" She asked, as she removed the blood soaked handkerchief from my wounds. "It's still bleeding, but its not as bad as it was."

She gently cleaned the congealed blood away, so that she could get a better look at how bad the cuts were. There was a large lump where the bottle had struck, and several cuts to the surrounding area, the largest of which continued to ooze blood.

"This should be stitched." She insisted, getting up to leave the room.

"Where are you going?" I asked, concerned that she was going to phone the doctor.

"To get some bandages."

Jackie returned a couple of minutes later, and cut up a square of lint dressing which she pressed to the wound, sending a piercing pain through the back of my head.

"Hold that there while I clean you up." She began wiping away the blood stains from my cheek. Streaks of blood had run from the back of my head, around my ear and across my cheek, while others had run down my neck and round across my chin and throat.

"God, this is going to take ages." She cursed.

A woman of about fifty years of age came through into the kitchen. She was well built and fairly tall, with blonde hair tinged grey, and piercing green eyes.

"Hi, mum." Jackie looked up and smiled. "This is Mike, remember I told you about him."

"Hello." I said timidly, feeling very awkward about my appearance.

"In trouble again are you." The woman frowned. "That's typical."

"It wasn't our fault, mum." Jackie explained calmly, still wiping the blood away from my face.

"Oh no. It never is, is it?" Her mother shook her head in disapproval.

"What's that mean?" Jackie asked calmly. "I've never brought any trouble home, and you know it."

"Huh! You think I don`t know what you get up to working in that pub." Her mother wagged her finger at her, and scowled. "Don`t try to kid me that you're an innocent little girl, because I know better. You can't pull the wool over my eyes."

I couldn't believe my ears to hear her mother talking to her in such a manner. Jackie looked at me in embarrassment.

"Oh mum really. Stop treating me like a child. There's nothing wrong with working in a pub. I earn good money, and it gives me something to do. You should be glad that I'm working, most of my friends can't get jobs."

"Friends? What friends?" Her mother turned and left as abruptly as she had entered.

"Are you okay?" I put my hand up and stroked Jackie's cheek to comfort her. She was clearly upset by the remarks, but tried hard not to show it.

"Yes, of course." Jackie shrugged. "She's just annoyed that I brought you home."

"I shouldn't have come here?" I felt guilty at having been the cause of such a spiteful attack.

"Of course you should." Jackie went back to the task of cleaning my face. "I had to bring you here to make sure that you're okay. That's more important to me than whether or not my mother feels put out about it. Do you know, whenever I ask her if she minds me bringing friends back, she says she doesn't, but every time I do so, she reacts like this. She would have been the same if you weren't hurt, and we were just having a cup of tea together."

Jackie finished cleaning the blood from my face and neck, and then took away the dressing which I had been holding on the wound, so that she could see if it was still bleeding. She went away and came back with a sachet of powder which she opened, and sprinkled onto the wound.

"Are you sure you wouldn't prefer me to take you to the casualty?" She asked. "How do you feel?"

"I feel a lot better." I replied, feeling genuinely more refreshed at having had the dried blood cleaned away. "Let's see how I feel after another hour. Here, let me clean you up now. You have blood smudged on your face."

I took the cloth, and began to gently wipe her cheek with it. I felt a warm contented feeling just being close to her.

"There, that's better." I said as I finished wiping her cheek.

Jackie took another look at the wound on my head.

"It's just about stopped bleeding." She sprinkled a bit more powder onto it. "I daren't try to wash the blood from your hair in case I start it bleeding again."

I looked up at her as she frowned at the wound. "You're quite a little Florence Nightingale, aren't you?" I teased her, putting my arm around her waist, and holding her close. "Give me a kiss, and I'll feel much better."

Jackie laughed and put her arms around my shoulders, giving me a long, warm, affectionate kiss. I squeezed her tightly. I had completely forgotten about the pain. I just felt a deep sense of happiness and contentment, as I lay my head gently against her breast, and listened to her heart pounding away.

"Did you get my cigarettes?" A voice came from the doorway.

Jackie turned around, startled by the interruption. Her mother entered once more. "Em no, I'm afraid we didn't." Jackie hesitated to think. "Mike was getting them for me when he was attacked."

"Oh that's just great." Her mother rolled her eyes in annoyance. "I haven't got any left at all. Where am I supposed to get them from now?"

"Don't worry, I'll get you some when I take Mike home, okay." The tone of Jackie's voice indicated that she was beginning to lose her patience.

"Don't bother, I'll get them myself." Her mother muttered as she left the room once more. A couple of minutes later she went out, slamming the front door behind her.

Jackie held up her hands in despair. "God, she drives me nuts," she cursed. "You get yourself hurt whilst buying her damned cigarettes, and all she cares about is that you didn't bring them with you afterwards. I'm sorry she's been so rude."

"Hey, don't apologise." I tugged playfully on her gold chain belt, pulling her closer. "You did warn me what to expect. Look at the state I'm in. She probably thinks I've been brawling."

"But that's just the trouble, she thinks bad of everyone I know, and that's because she thinks bad of me. She's never been proud of me since the day I was born, and my dad's just as bad. I get the impression that they never really wanted any children, and that I've been in their way ever since they had me."

"It's probably just their way. They probably think the world of you, but find it hard to show it." I took hold of her hand and tried to comfort her, but she was still upset. It was clear that although she tried to hide her feelings, her parents' coldness affected her deeply.

"Maybe." Jackie shrugged her shoulders, but felt sure inside that it was not the case.

Apparently her parents had never shown her any real love, not even as a small child, and yet she continued to love them, which made it all the more difficult for her to bear. She had always sought their affection, and the harder she had tried, the further they had pushed her away. This had given her a lonely and insecure childhood, alleviated only by her uncle, who had felt her sorrow and treated her like a daughter. He had given her the love and affection that she had lacked from her parents, and when he had died the previous year, she had lost the only person that she had ever really felt close to.

As she dwelt on past heartaches, she felt a powerful feeling of belonging welling up inside of her, so much so that she flung her arms around me, and burst into tears.

"Don`t cry." I begged her, misunderstanding the reason for her tears. "I'm sure they don`t mean the things they say."

"It doesn't matter." She wiped away some tears, and broke into a smile. "I have you."

"Of course you do." I said with some surprise at her remark. "I love you."

As soon as the words slipped out, I cursed myself beneath my breath. It now seemed a silly thing to say. I had known her for less than a week, and now I was telling her that I loved her, like a bashful schoolboy on his first date.

"I love you, too." Jackie's words sent a cold tingling sensation through my whole body. I think even Jackie was surprised by the suddenness of her announcement.

"You needn't feel that you have to say that just because I did." I felt embarrassed at having put her on the spot.

"I know." Jackie got off her chair, and sat on my knee, resting her head on my shoulder.

I lifted her head from my shoulder, and kissed her passionately. Jackie immediately responded by opening her mouth slightly, and soon I felt her flickering tongue against the tip of mine. I put my hand behind her head and pulled her against me tightly, as I explored the deeper recesses of her warm sensuous mouth. I felt her heavy breath against my cheek, and her wild, probing fingers running up and down my back and shoulders. I looked at her tightly shut eyes, just the blue eye-shadow showing against her long blonde eye-lashes, and her pale smooth skin. I opened my hand, and ran it up her neck and through her hair, delighting in the sensation as the silky strands sliding between my fingers. I knew it excited her from the way she arched her back and tensed her neck.

Jackie broke away from the kiss, took a deep breath, and rested her head back on my shoulders. We sat quietly, enjoying the feeling of being so close to each other, physically and emotionally, until Jackie finally broke the silence.

"Most of my other boyfriends were too full of themselves. I hate men who show off and try to be macho. Do you know what I mean?"

"I guess so."

"I better clean you up a bit more before you go home." She got up, and fetched some more hot water. Much of the blood had dried into my hair by now, and despite attempts to soften it up with the water, some bits would not come out. In the end Jackie had to cut quite a bit of my hair away to remove the last traces of blood. She stepped back to look at the results.

"That's the best I can do with it." She shook her head and grinned. "Well you can see why I'm a barmaid and not a hair-dresser. Still, at least the bleeding hasn't started again. How do you feel?"

"I feel okay. Well, better than okay. I feel great with you next to me." I had a rather dreamy gaze across my face, and began tugging playfully on her belt to draw her near again.

"Be serious for a minute." Jackie tried hard to be stern. "You've had a bad knock. I have to be sure that you're okay before I take you home. Do you have a headache, or strange vision?"

"No. The only pain is from the lump on my head, and from my ribs where I was kicked." I tried to be serious.

"Your ribs?" Jackie exclaimed. "What's wrong with your ribs?"

"Oh, nothing much. They kicked me a couple of times while I was on the floor."

"Let me take a look." Jackie insisted, and began to loosen my shirt.

"It's nothing really." I protested, but made no attempt to stop her. Sure enough there were several areas of severe bruising, but nothing seemed to be broken.

"If you start getting any headaches or any other problems once you get home, you will call a doctor won't you?"

"Yes, okay." I nodded convincingly.

The front door opened as Jackie's mother returned with her cigarettes.

"Come on, let's go." Jackie made her way towards the door, and I followed, tucking my shirt back in. Jackie's mother gave me a scowl as I did so, but I ignored it and left. We looked at each other as we walked out to the car, and burst into laughter simultaneously. It was obvious what her mother had thought, but what the heck.

"I think I made a good impression with your mother, don't you?" I chuckled sarcastically, as I got into the car.

"You won't be on her Christmas card list, that's for sure." Jackie smiled back. "But then neither am I, so who cares?"

Jackie drove me back to the shops, where she had picked me up what seemed like an eternity ago.

"Shall I see you on Wednesday?" I asked.

"Sure. I sometimes go to the sports centre to play badminton during the week. Do you fancy going?"

"Umm, I suppose so." I hesitated, and then with more enthusiasm, "Yes sure, I'll give it a try."

"I'll meet you here at seven o'clock."

I gave her one last lingering kiss, and let her drive away. I watched her car speed away down the road and disappear out of sight before turning to walk the hundred yards or so back home. As I started walking, I began to realise that I was a lot less stable on my feet than I had thought. Jackie was gone, so I was alone.

I sat down on a low wall and tried to clear my head which had begun spinning. After a few minutes rest, I was able to carry on for a few more yards, and eventually I made it home with a number of stops. By now my head was thumping severely. I climbed up the stairs and lay down on the bed, still fully clothed. I remembered my promise to call a doctor, and lay there trying to decide whether I should. The next thing I knew it was morning, and all I felt was the pain from my cuts and bruises.

CHAPTER FOUR

July 1975: As the months drifted by, Jackie and I continued to see each other whenever we could, and our affection grew ever deeper. Jackie's interest in badminton had turned me into an enthusiast also. In addition to improving my fitness, it had enabled me to share in something which Jackie really enjoyed. Jackie had also started giving me driving lessons, and I ended up doing most of the driving wherever we went, so as to get practice.

With the arrival of the summer holidays, I went away with my family to our caravan in mid-Wales. I had just turned seventeen, and had traded in my moped for a real motorcycle. Instead of going to the caravan in the car with the rest of my family, I went separately on my motorcycle.

This turned out to be more of an adventure than I had planned. Within an hour of setting off on the journey, I was stung on my neck by a wasp. That in itself was nothing extraordinary, so I continued on my way, but about an hour and a half later I became aware that something was crawling around on my chest. I stopped at the roadside and began stripping off in haste, much to the surprise of passing motorists. The wasp stung me four more times before I finally evicted it from my clothing.

Despite having been stung five times, I resisted the temptation to kill it. Proof indeed that I was a budding conservationist even then. On reflection I probably did it no favours, since it would have had a tough task finding its way back home some 60 miles away.

This had been the first time since our first meeting almost a year before, that Jackie and I had been separated for more than a few days. It seemed like an eternity. Nevertheless it was a good holiday, as our family holidays always were, and eventually the time did pass. My family returned home so that my father could return to work, but being a student I had lots of holiday, and was able to stay on at the caravan for a couple of extra weeks. Needless to say, it was not long after my family's departure that Jackie arrived to join me, and I was waiting to greet her with open arms.

I showed her around the caravan, which owing to its compact size did not take long, but the caravan was well equipped, and very comfortable. It was in fact only a couple of years old, having replaced an early caravan that had been blown half way up the hill during a ferocious storm.

"Come on, lets go and get some food." Jackie picked up her car keys from the kitchen table, and waved me towards the door.

"Shall I drive?" I asked, making my way out towards the car.

"Of course." Jackie threw me the car keys.

By the time we had eaten and returned to the caravan, it was already quite late. There was a small bar on the caravan park which we decided to try, and by the time we arrived, it was not far off closing time. We went in, bought drinks, and sat down at the table in the corner. It was a very small club indeed, with only about eight tables, a juke box and a one-armed bandit. Even so it was cosy, and it was so close that we could walk home in a couple of minutes.

"I know it sounds corny, but I felt quite lost without you." Jackie confessed to me. "I wasn't able to settle to anything, and kept wondering what you were doing."

"I can tell you that". I took a sip of my drink. "I was counting down the days until today, that's what. But it's funny really, because last year when I hadn't met you, I did the same things here with my family, and never wanted to leave."

I took hold of her hand and interlaced my fingers with hers, squeezing tightly. "God, I do love you. I won't go away like that again, I promise"

"Hey, don't make promises." She put her arm around my shoulder, and gave me a kiss on the cheek.

"Is that all I get?" I teased her. "After two weeks apart?"

"Until later, yes." She gave me a wicked, inviting smile.

"Now who's making promises?" I joked back.

"It was only two weeks." Jackie sipped her drink casually. "Anyway, it doesn't harm to be reminded that you miss me."

"It's strange," I said as I slid my hands around her slender waist. "I always thought I would be about twenty five years old, and in my chosen career by the time I got seriously involved with a girl."

"Oh, that's how you think of me, is it?" Jackie asked.

"How do you mean?"

"Seriously involved."

"Of course." I assured her, surprised by the question. "I love you very much, you must know that, don't you?"

"Yes," She nodded. "It's just nice to hear you say it, that's all."

"I know it sounds soppy, but I never knew what love meant until I met you." I ran my hand behind her head and held her gently against my chest.

"That's hardly surprising. You were only sixteen."

"Yes I suppose." I nodded, and took another sip of my drink. "But there are things that I do with you that make me turn to jelly. Things I would never have thought of as being sensual."

"Like what?"

I began to feel embarrassed, and wished I'd never started this line of discussion.

"Like holding hands with you palm to palm, like this." I took hold of her hand, and held it flat against mine, sliding my palm against hers. Then I interlacing my fingers with hers, and squeezing her hand tightly.

"What else?" She asked.

"This." I put my hand on the back of her neck, and ran my open fingers up through her hair, so that I could feel her scalp under my palm, and the strands of hair sliding softly through my fingers. Jackie closed her eyes, and began arching her head back from the sensation.

"What else?" Jackie repeated, her eyes still closed from the sensation she was experiencing.

"Running my fingers over your lips." I put my index finger against her slightly parted lips, and began running it along them gently. "And along your teeth."

She parted her lips further, and I accepted the invitation, and started running my finger along the front of her closed teeth. I put my finger between her teeth, and gently prised them open, so that I could run my fingers between them. I could feel her hot breath against my palm, and then the tip of her tongue brushing against my finger. Gently I put my finger deeper into her mouth, and she responded by running her tongue up and down my finger. She closed her teeth gently around it, and sucked. The smooth, warm, wet feel of her mouth around my finger sent shivers down my spine.

"And what your doing now." I sighed. "I wouldn't have believed that it could feel so good."

Jackie slid her lips off my finger and looked up at me almost in a state of trance. "I never thought I'd ever meet someone I felt like this about." She put her arm around my neck and pulled me towards her waiting lips. She kissed me passionately, her silky wet lips pressed tightly against mine, and her slippery tongue darting in and out of my mouth.

"Why have you never asked me to make love to you?" Jackie asked boldly.

I was surprised by the question. "Should I have done?" I asked hesitantly.

"Yes."

I starred into her sparkling blue eyes; my heart pounding with excitement.

"Let's go home." I suggested, holding my hand out across the table. She took my hand, and rose to her feet.

We strolled out into the cool starry night, and walked arm in arm back to the caravan, neither of us saying a word. When we reached the caravan, I opened the door for her to enter, and followed her inside. I lit one of the gas lamps, and turned to her in the pale orange light.

I put my arms around her waist, and held her tightly against me. Our lips were only an inch apart, as we breathed heavily with excitement. I could feel her hot breath as I inhaled; it was like her soul entering my body. I pulled her lips against me once more, sliding my hands down her back. I felt the graceful curves of her waist beneath her silky white blouse, and brought my hands to rest against the belt of her tightly fitting skirt. I longed to slide them on down, so that I could feel her body through the smooth cotton of her black skirt.

Jackie broke away from the kiss, and led me into the bedroom by the hand. Arm in arm we lay back onto the bed, with Jackie on top of me, so that we were once again face to face. She raised herself up slightly on her elbows, and I parted my legs so that she slid down between them, sending an ecstatic tingle through my groins. I looked up at her, but was not able to see her eyes in the semi-darkness. All that I could see was her outline, and her hair glistening in what light there was.

"You mean the world to me." I tightened my grip around her waist. "If I'd never met you, I might never have known what love is. I might never have known what I was missing. But now I do know. Things could never go back to how they were. I'd rather die than loose you, now."

"You won't ever loose me." She kissed me on the fore ead. "I'm yours forever. I promise."

I kissed her on her throat, an act which awakened primitive feelings of trust and desire within her. I slid my hand up her back, and across under her arm, until it brushed against the side of her breast. I then ran my palm gently across the front of her blouse, feeling the firm roundness of her breast beneath her blouse. She remained motionless, and said nothing. Gingerly I began to undo one of the buttons of her blouse, half expecting her to stop me, but she didn't.

I undid all the buttons, and slid my hand inside her blouse, and up her back to feel for her bra clasp. As I had half expected, she pulled away from me, but instead of stopping me, she sat up and opened her bra from the front. I gently slid my hands across her quivering stomach: her skin feeling like satin beneath my palms. I felt the ripples of her ribs as I moved on upwards, her chest heaving as she drew breath. Finally I felt the soft rounded skin of her breasts, and ran my fingers around them, cradling them in my hands.

She ran her hands across my chest, and began to undo my shirt. She slid her hands up and down my naked chest, and then ran her nails across me gently, causing me to tense up from the strangely exciting sensation. She bent down and kissed my chest, before closing her teeth gently around the skin. I groaned softly, and brought my hands down behind her head to hold her tightly against my chest.

She slid her way slowly up my chest, and then gave me a long lingering kiss on the lips. I leaned forward slightly, and placed my lips to her breast. She put her arms around me, and supported me as I gently explored her smooth silky skin.

I ran my hands down over her hips, and felt the folds of material from her skirt which had ridden up as she sat astride me. I slid my hands down towards her thighs, until I felt the soft silky touch of her tights. She squeezed her knees together, pressing them into my sides, and sighed. I transferred my kisses from her soft rounded breasts, to the warm valley between them. I ran my tongue up between them; it tasted salty. Exquisite.

By now Jackie was gripping my head tightly, and running her fingers through my hair in erratic jerky movements. I caressed her inner thighs firmly, and felt her hips rocking backwards and forwards ever so slightly, in rhythm with my caresses. Her breathing had become deep and erratic, and her knees dug ever more tightly into my sides. Jackie threw her head back and groaned softly, her knees gripping my sides so tightly that I thought my ribs would break.

"Just a minute." She stopped and got up to remove the remainder of her clothing. I also removed my clothing, but with less dignity and composure than Jackie had done. I slowly pulled her back down onto the bed, and kissed her deeply and passionately. Her hair fell forward against my face, and her hips pressed against mine. Jackie's nails dug into my back, but the pain merely heightened my desire. She moaned something to me, but I couldn't tell what it was. My mind drifted in and out of reality, as I floated on a cocktail of physical desire and spiritual unity, the likes of which I had never felt before.

I pressed my lips against hers once more, and hugged her ever so tightly, as if to make myself as close to her physically as I felt emotionally. I felt my very soul becoming one with hers, as we consummated our relationship. An emotion so strong that it made me light-headed, and my head fell back, breaking our kiss. Again she dug her nails into me, gripping me tightly with her arms and knees. She pulled my head back up towards her, and I felt her hot panting breath against my neck, as her body went limp in my arms.

I lay motionless, holding her in my arms and dwelling on the emotions of what had taken place. Whenever I looked at Jackie, I felt physically attracted to her slender curvaceous body, her beautiful blue eyes, and her gorgeous blonde hair, but at the time of lovemaking I had barely noticed any of that. The powerful emotions had come from something much deeper, much more fundamental. Emotions that I had never felt before. That this was real love could not be doubted. Compared to these emotions, nothing else in life mattered; not studying, not money, not motorcycles, not anything.

A sniffle alerted me to the fact that Jackie was crying.

"What's wrong?" I asked, fearing that I had done something wrong. Maybe I had got too carried away, and rushed her too fast. "Didn't you want to do that?"

"Of course." She kissed my neck.

"What's wrong then?" I was confused, and concerned.

"Was that your first time?" She asked.

I suddenly felt a fear welling up inside of me.

"Yes." I replied reluctantly. "Was it that obvious?"

"No." Jackie reassured me. "But it wasn't mine........ and it should have been."

I didn't really know how to answer that. It didn't matter to me that she had had previous boyfriends, or that she had made love with them. Since she was several years older than I was, I rather expected it.

"Its the present that's important." I finally answered. "And the future."

"Yes I know." She sniffled and forced a smile, but I could not see the smile in the semi darkness. She kissed me tenderly on the cheek, and slid off me.

She unzipped the double sleeping bag so that we could actually get into it, rather than just lie on top of it, and we snuggled back together again. We lay together side by side, arm in arm, neither uttering a word. We merely savoured the sensation of being close to each other, and floated off to sleep on a cloud of love and security.

CHAPTER FIVE

July 1976: The pressures of study had grown progressively as I had neared my A' level examinations, but I had always made sure that I did not let them interfere with my relationship with Jackie. I knew that she was far more important to my future well-being, than my studies ever could. I also knew that my parents would never have seen things the same way. For that very reason I had kept my relationship with Jackie a secret, with the help of a school-friend called John, who shared my interest in motorcycles.

During the previous Christmas I had tried to tell my parents about Jackie, partly because I had wanted her to be with me over Christmas, but somehow the time had never seemed appropriate. As our relationship continued to blossom, it became increasingly obvious that I must come clean with my parents, since it was becoming more and more difficult to justify why I hadn't told them. I promised Jackie that I would tell them on my eighteenth birthday, by which time I would have finished my A' levels, and would be in a position to plan my future.

Prior to my birthday however, my parents had begun making radical plans to give up their work in Manchester, and move to Wales to buy a craft shop business. I was left in two minds as to whether I should remain in Manchester, or move to Wales with my family.

Had I not been planning to go to university, I would have remained in Manchester with Jackie, but in view of the fact that I would only be in Wales for the summer holidays, I decided to go with them. This was probably the hardest decision I ever had to make in my life. The six weeks I was to be apart from Jackie seemed like an eternity.

Jackie and I agreed that as soon as I knew which university I was going to, she would make plans to move there for the beginning of term, so that we could live together. She was keen to go, and saw it as her opportunity to move away from home. I was delighted that she had decided to do this, and felt in my heart that

Mike Bingham

we would always be together as a couple from here on, whatever the future held in store for us.

It was a tearful farewell the day I finally left Manchester, and moved to the small Welsh village of Bethesda. I felt a great forbidding, as though I would never see Jackie again. I knew that I was being silly, but was still unable to shake off this awful fear. I almost turned back, so great was this fear.

When my exam results finally came through, I was very disappointed. The results reflected the lack of work that I had put in, and I was unable to get a place at any of the universities. I was however able to get a place at Lanchester Polytechnic in Coventry, to study Biology. As it turned out, this was not a bad choice, since it was reasonably accessible from both Wales and Manchester.

As soon as I had secured my place at Lanchester Polytechnic, I rode down to Manchester on my Kawasaki 350 to see Jackie. She ran out from the house, and leapt into my arms before I had even had a chance to remove my helmet.

"Oh, Mike" She pulled my helmet off, almost taking my ears with it. "I've missed you so much."

I put my arms around her and squeezed her so tightly that she gasped.

"There were times when I wondered if I would ever see you." I admitted.

"Don't be so silly." She dragged me into the house by the arm. "My parents have gone out."

"Did they know I was coming?" I felt compelled to ask.

"Yes. I expect that's why they went out." She grinned. "Are you hungry? Do you want some food before we go?"

"No, I stopped at a cafe only an hour ago." I put my arms around her waist, and pulled her close. "But I do want another kiss."

She responded with a passionate kiss and embrace, before pulling away to get her leather jacket.

"Are we still going on your motorbike?" She asked excitedly.

"Sure, if your still keen."

"Yes, great. Let's go."

We rode down to Coventry on my motorcycle, and booked into a hotel. We registered as a married couple, and took a double room. Jackie went up to the room to take a shower, while I went to a nearby newsagents to buy a collection of local papers, which I took back to our room. I let myself in with the key she had left in the door.

"I've got quite a few." I announced as I closed the door.

"Good, we'll look at them later." Jackie was undressed and snuggled up in the large double bed. "I'm cold. Come and keep me warm."

I needed no further invitation. I had already waited long enough to be alone with her. After an hour of passionate love-making, we lay arm in arm in a state of blissful exhaustion.

Jackie threw the bedclothes to one side, and let out a sigh.

"I thought you were cold?" I teased.

"I was, and now I'm hot." She reached across and picked up one of the papers that I had bought. "Okay, let's see what's on offer."

We sat in bed together, looking through the small ads for accommodation to let, and putting circles around half a dozen that looked of interest.

"There are more than I'd expected." I said, putting the telephone on the bed in front of us.

"You don't think it's too late to phone now?" Jackie looked at her watch; it was a little after ten o'clock.

"No. I'd rather wake someone up, than risk being beaten to it by someone else"

I phoned up four of the most promising, to make appointments to view them the following day. One of the four had already been let that afternoon, but that still left three of interest to view.

I replaced the phone, and we snuggled up face to face. I put one arm over her waist, and the other under her neck and around her shoulders, so that her head was half supported by my arm, and half by the pillow. We had learned that this was the most comfortable way to sleep arm in arm. Never has one slept the sleep of angels, until one sleeps in the arms of their true love.

In the morning we set off to view the flats that we had selected, but the bike developed a serious misfire. It appeared as though the piston rings had gone on one of the cylinders. We were able to make all the appointments, but I doubted that the bike would get us home.

By far the best flat we saw was the second one, and we returned to confirm that we would take it, and put down a deposit. It was nicely decorated and furnished, and had everything we needed. It wasn't very big, but that didn't matter for the two of us.

With the flat now reserved, it only remained to get the bike sorted out during the afternoon, so that we could return home the following day. As it turned out, the local bike shop was very impressed by my Kawasaki, since it was an early rotary-disc valve models: quite a collector's item in fact. I was offered a straight swap for a much newer Benelli 250. I was fairly happy with the deal, and it did solve our problem.

We had one last night of romance at the hotel, and then returned to Manchester the following morning. After another tearful farewell, I returned to Bethesda alone. The two days I spent with Jackie had flown by all too quickly, but it would not be long until we were re-united in Coventry once more.

CHAPTER SIX

September 1976: The days passed by, and eventually I arrived in Coventry, eager to start my degree course in biology, and even more eager to see Jackie again. I had been allocated a room in the student's accommodation at Priory Hall, a huge tower block adjacent to the Polytechnic, over-looking the bus station. Visitors were not allowed in the student's accommodation, so I spent most of my time in Jackie's flat. She had arrived a couple of weeks ahead of me, and had already found work in a burger-bar, just a few hundred metres from Priory Hall. Things had worked out perfectly, and by incredible coincidence, my old school-friend John Harris also ended up in Coventry at the same polytechnic.

I soon made new friends amongst the people on my course, and amongst my fellow occupants of Priory Hall. Two of these held strong religious beliefs, and before long we became involved in some fairly deep discussions about religion. I had attended church regularly as a child, but had never really given much thought to religion, or to the existence of God. I had routinely attended church with my mother because it was expected of me. Now for the first time, I began to think seriously about Christianity.

Ever since my first premonition as a child, I had been convinced that there was more to life than what we could physically sense. The more I discussed religion with my friends, the more convinced I became that God was the answer. For the first time in several years I began praying and reading the bible. I prayed for love, friendship and family, rather than wealth and status which did not interest me. I also prayed that my education would lead me to a career which would be spiritually fulfilling, rather than financially rewarding. I thanked God for the blessings I had been given, particularly for Jackie who was my life. I prayed for our future marriage and family life. Little did I know that the very blessings for which I was giving praise were soon to be torn from me in the most brutal and horrific manner.

Despite my new found belief in God, my interest in motorcycles remained undiminished, and I had managed to save quite a lot of money working in

Bethesda over the summer. Jackie was also in secure employment again, and following her first experience of motorcycles a few weeks earlier, she had become hooked on them. I regretted swapping my Kawasaki for the smaller Benelli, which was a bit slow with the added weight of a passenger. We therefore decided to purchase a larger bike, and after much consideration, we decided to look for a Triumph Bonneville or a Norton Commando.

There was very little choice locally, but we found a bike which sounded absolutely ideal advertised in Motorcycle News. The only problem was that it was in Southampton. After thinking about it for a while, we decided that it was worth making the journey down to see it. If it turned out to be no good, then we would simply have a day out in Southampton instead.

On the 23rd of October, we drove down to Southampton in Jackie's car, and arrived there mid-afternoon. As soon as we saw the bike, we both fell in love with it. It was bright yellow with black coach-lining. The tank and seat were sculptured along the lines of a Grand Prix racer, and it had a full Barcelona fairing with twin headlights. It was an absolute beauty, and I bought it for the princely sum of £450.

At first I had trouble handling the bike, especially around the streets of Southampton. The Triumph was not only larger and more powerful than the Benelli, but the racing style handlebars were very low down, and completely different from anything I had previously ridden. Out on the open road however, the bike really came into its own, and I was exhilarated by the surge of power that accompanied every tweak of the throttle.

Jackie followed behind in the Capri, wishing that she could be on the bike with me.

Shortly before Winchester, I pulled into a service station to fill up with petrol. Jackie pulled up behind me at the pumps, but did not need fuel. I filled the tank, and went to pay at the kiosk. A Ford Escort with four men pulled up behind Jackie's car, and they began to get impatient because nobody was using the pump. Once they realised that there was a young attractive girl alone in the car, their attitude changed, and they began taunting her with sexist remarks and gestures. As I was waiting to pay, I noticed that they were up to something, so I jumped the queue and put a five pound note on the counter to pay for the fuel.

Not realising that I was with Jackie, they continued taunting her as I approached. My blood began to boil, as anger took over from reason.

Jackie got out of the car, and came across to cut me off before I even reached the vehicles.

"They're just drunk Mike. Forget it." She put her arms around me to calm me down, and that did the trick, as she knew it would. She was of course right, as always, but it still made me angry.

It wasn't long before it was getting dusk, and I put my headlights on. As I began slowing down for an approaching roundabout, I became aware of headlights other than my own lighting up the road in front. I turned to see what was happening, but too late. Jackie's car nudged me in the rear, sending me into a slide.

I partially corrected the slide, but as I did so the wheels of my bike ran up against the kerb of the roundabout, and I was catapulted into the grass. I felt a violent jarring to my head which left me completely dazed.

Jackie screeched to a halt and leapt out of the car, shouting abuse at the men in the Ford Escort. They had deliberately rammed into the back of her, causing her in turn to run into me.

"Are you okay Mike?" She asked as she rushed across to help me up.

My mind was spinning in a vortex of confusion and pain. I remember Jackie helping me up into a sitting position, and I remember the horror on her face as she removed my helmet and saw the extent of my injuries.

"Oh my God." She burst out in fear and shock at the horrendous injuries that befell her eyes. She began to shake and cry, and even in my dazed state I knew that it was bad.

Two men suddenly grabbed Jackie's arms and dragged her to her feet, leaving me still sitting up in the long grass.

"Over there." A third man pointed. The three of them then dragged her towards a gateway as she continued to stare at me helplessly.

I knew that I had to help her, so I manoeuvred myself onto all fours in an attempt to get to my feet. As I looked down, I could see a stream of blood trickling onto the ground from my face. My whole arm was covered with warm sticky blood. I remained frozen for a moment, staring down at the small pool of blood as it gradually spread out, increasing in size. To my eternal shame, my mind abandoned all thoughts of Jackie's plight: I knew that with injuries this bad, I was probably dying. My arms began to tremble, and I fell face down into the grass.

Shouting and screaming from across the road reminded me once more of the need to help Jackie. It occurred to me that if I could get out of the long grass and onto the road, a passing motorist might see me and stop to help. I tried once again to get up onto all fours, but my strength had abandoned me. Whether it was from blood loss, shock, or just the realisation that my injuries were so grave, I do not know.

The three men had lifted Jackie over a wooden gate, and dropped her onto the ground behind a hedge, where they could not be seen. She did not fight them, but remained motionless with tears streaming down her cheeks. One of the men pulled her jacket and blouse open, ripping off the buttons in the process. A second man bent down, and placed a knife to the centre of her chest. In one violent stroke he cut through her bra to reveal her naked breasts.

They pulled open her jeans, and tugged them down over her legs so violently, that her legs and back were lifted clean off the ground, but still the jeans would not come over her ankles.

"Never mind that." The man said, cutting through her knickers with his knife. With his trousers already down around his knees, he began forcing himself between her thighs.

Jackie stared at him coldly through her tear-filled eyes, and smelt the stink of booze on his breathe, but she feel somehow remote from what was happening. She was aware of the ruthless act that was taking place, but it was as though it was happening to someone else, and she was viewing from afar.

As the second man took his turn at Jackie, a passing motorist pulled up alongside the parked cars. The fourth man had stayed by the cars, as if trying to distance himself from the repulsive act that his friends were performing.

"What can I do to help?" The driver asked through his wound-down window.

The fourth man hesitated before replying, "Find the nearest phonebox, and call for an ambulance."

I cannot say whether this was a genuine attempt to summon help, or merely a means of getting the motorist to leave before he discovered what was really happening. In any case, the car sped away, and I knew that help would eventually come.

The fourth man went across to the gate, and shouted to his friends. "Come on, we've got to go. There's an ambulance on its way."

The third man finished his business, and zipped up his pants. They hopped back over the gate, laughing and jeering, got back into the car and drove off.

Jackie lifted herself up onto her knees, and then onto her feet. The semen ran down her thighs, and she wiped it away with the remains of her knickers, before throwing them angrily into the hedge. She pulled up the jeans that were still stuck around her ankles, so that she was able to walk, and made her way towards the gate as fast as her wobbly legs would allow.

The tears continued to stream down her cheeks, and she began to wipe them away, but as she did so she smelt the repulsive odour of semen on her hands.

Nausea welled up inside of her, and she vomited violently, supporting herself against the gate.

Trying to regain her thoughts as best she could, she climbed over the gate, and hurried across the road to reach me. She kneeled down beside me, and carefully lifted me back up into a sitting position, cradling my bleeding head in her arms.

"Mike, can you hear me?" A familiar voice floated through my foggy mind.

"Yes." The single word sent a piercing pain through my head, and I recoiled violently.

"Steady. Don't try to talk." Jackie's soothing voice helped me to get a grip on where I was, and what was happening. She tore off a section of her tattered blouse, and wrapped it around my forehead to stem the bleeding.

"What did they do to you?" I asked, prepared for the pain of talking this time.

"Nothing that a hot shower won't put right." Jackie answered calmly. "I'm okay. It's you that they've hurt."

"I'm sorry." I sobbed, the tears stinging the wounds on my face.

"For what?" Jackie shook her head, and began to cry too. "I'm the one who should say sorry. Look what they've done to you. Don't you dare die on me. I need you. You're all I have."

I tried to say that it wasn't her fault, and not to worry, but I could not get any more words out. There was so much that I wanted to tell her. I just hoped that she knew already.

I lay against her, and tried to calm myself as best I could. The pain was growing in intensity minute by minute. As I breathed in and out, I became aware that my breath was bubbling out of my eye socket, accompanied by a sickly sound. I couldn't see anything with my right eye, and it was obvious that my skull was badly smashed.

My jaw hurt terribly, and as I probed the roof of my mouth with my tongue, I began to realise that half of my palate was missing. The upper row of teeth were no longer pointing downwards on the right hand side, but were pointing across. It soon became apparent that the whole section of bone supporting the teeth, including the roof of my mouth, had sheared off and turned through 90°. I now knew why my breathing was passing in and out of my eye socket. I knew from my studies of human biology that the roof of the mouth was an integral part of the nasal passages and the eye socket. No wonder I couldn't see. The whole side of my skull had been smashed to a pulp.

My self-assessment of the situation was not far from the mark. The bones which made up the roof of my mouth, my cheek and my eye socket, had indeed been completely smashed away on the right side of my face. My nose had been completely severed off, and was dangling by a small strip of skin. The bone around the eye socket had been destroyed, and my right eye was hanging out, held only by its muscle and nerve attachments.

I had no doubt in my mind that I was dying, and I knew that Jackie thought so too. Her eyes were filled with fear, her lips trembled, and the tears continued to stream down her face. I tried to tell her that I loved her, but I couldn't speak. I squeezed her hand tightly, and she reciprocated. Our entwined fingers were coated in half-dried blood, making them stick together.

Even though I thought I was dying, I felt strangely calm. I knew that Jackie would stay with me until the end came. I wanted to feel her lips against mine one last time, but my injuries made that impossible. I felt waves of tranquillity washing over me, and the dreadful pain began to slowly subside. I began to feel almost comfortable, cradled in the arms of my true-love: my soul-mate. The sickly sweet smell of blood had gone, and all I could smell was Jackie's favourite perfume. My grip on her hand began to slacken, and I let myself float off into a peaceful dream-world.

"Mike!" Jackie screamed at me, bringing me back to the world of pain and fear. "Don't you dare give up."

The dreadful pain made me cry out, and the smell of blood made me feel nauseous. I realised how terribly cold I felt, but I wasn't shivering.

"Keep squeezing my hand." Jackie comforted me, altering her grip on me slightly.

I did as she asked and squeezed her hand again.

"If you give up, you'll die. You mustn't do that." Her voice was full of panic. "I need you."

"Keep talking to him." I heard another voice that I didn't recognise, and I realised that we were not alone.

"I know you're uncomfortable, but I've got to keep you upright to slow down the blood loss." Jackie's familiar voice continued. "You can make it, but you've got to fight. You've lost a lot of blood. I know you feel weak and tired, but you mustn't sleep. If you do you'll never wake. You've got so much to live for. We have all our lives ahead of us. What am I going to do without you?"

Jackie broke down into tears again.

"I love you." I forced the words through the pain barrier, and squeezed her hand even tighter.

"The ambulance is here." A voice came from behind.

"Thank God." Jackie took a few deep breaths to stop the tears. "You'll be okay now. Help is here."

One of the ambulance man knelt down behind us, and removed the material that Jackie had been holding over the wounds. He placed a proper dressing around my whole head.

"Okay, we're going to lift him onto the stretcher." The ambulance driver informed Jackie.

"I'm coming with him." She insisted, as she reluctantly let go of my hand.

They lifted me onto the stretcher, and put me into the back of the ambulance. A moment later I heard the door close behind me. I was given an injection, presumably to ease the pain, and the ambulance began to move off.

I could see nothing, and felt very alone. It was a great relief to hear Jackie's voice once more, and to feel her taking hold of my hand. I felt so relieved to know that she was still with me. I had no fear of death, in fact the act of dying could be no worse than what I had already experienced. I felt so ill, and in such awful pain, that death itself could hold no greater torment.

Death was simply the end. The end of the pain, the end of self-consciousness, the end of my being with Jackie.

As my mind began to wander, it was not my past that flashed before me, but my future. I began to see my wedding to Jackie, the day I had longed for, with all my family able to share my joy at being with the woman I loved. I saw our first house together, and then I saw the birth of our baby girl. Small and helpless, covered in blood and mucus, I watched it draw its first breath of life. Jackie's hair was longer now, but her eyes held the same sparkle, as our baby was laid in her arms. I watched it take its first steps, its first day at school, its first broken heart. Her name was Sophie. I watched the pride in Jackie's eyes, as Jackie's mother played with Sophie; her precious grandchild. The gulf between mother and daughter finally closed by a grand-daughter. I watched as Sophie married, and saw my gracefully ageing wife playing with our grandchild.

Suddenly it all came to an abrupt end as the bubble burst, and I realised that this was not my future, just a dream. My realisation of the reality of death. The pain of death was not physical, it lay much deeper.

"Oh Jackie, I don't want to die." I burst into tears, and wept uncontrollably.

"You won't, you won't. I promise" She put her arm around my waist, and lay her head on my chest. I put my arm around her. I wished that I could see her and kiss her one last time, but somehow I knew it was not to be. I stroked her hair, which was matted with dried blood.

"Mike, promise me something." Jackie spoke softly. "Never tell anyone what they did to us tonight. It was a traffic accident, okay? Nothing else, just a traffic accident."

"Okay". I squeezed her hand to acknowledge her, and stroked her hair tenderly. My injuries were visible, but clearly Jackie had also suffered grave injuries, injuries that were much less visible.

Our embrace was shattered by the door bursting open, and my stretcher being whisked out by several hospital porters. I was rushed through into an operating theatre, where the bandages were removed from my head. In the bright lights of the theatre, I was able to make out a blurry image of people in white coats rushing around.

The pain had become unbearable, and I tried to ask for something to ease it, but the nurse could not understand me. She put her ear closer to me to listen.

"He's asking for something for the pain." She turned to the doctor.

"I'm sorry, but we can't let you have anything until the surgeon arrives." He told me coldly.

I lay facing upwards at the bright lights above me for what seemed an eternity. In reality it was a little under two hours. More than long enough to endure such pain. Finally I was informed that a specialist surgeon had arrived from Southampton to operate, and that I was finally to be given an injection to send me to sleep.

This was it. My heart began pounding frantically as I felt the cold liquid entering my arm. I would never wake again, my injuries were too grave. If one could ever experience the actual moment of death, it would be now, as I felt my last seconds of consciousness fading away. I felt a strange humming noise in my head, and then darkness fell.

The nurse brought Jackie a cup of coffee, and sat down beside her.

"Why don't you tell me what really happened?" She asked Jackie in a sympathetic, probing tone. "This was no ordinary accident. I can tell that from your clothes."

"I tore my blouse to stop the blood." Jackie insisted.

"What, and your bra too?" The nurse put her hand on Jackie's shoulder to comfort her. "Whatever you tell me is in strictest confidence, I promise."

Jackie looked up at her, trying to decide what she should tell her; whether she could trust her.

"You promise? Strictest confidence? You won't tell anyone?"

"No dear, not if that's what you want. I only want to help as best I can." Her charming manner convinced Jackie that she could trust her, and she explained in detail the events of the evening.

"You can't just ignore something like that." The nurse was shocked that Jackie did not want to report the incident. "You must report it."

"You don't understand. I can't tell anyone." Jackie felt very isolated by her decision.

"Why? You have nothing to be ashamed of. On the contrary, you handled yourself with great composure and dignity."

"I don't want anyone to know, that's all." Jackie looked down at her coffee. Tears rolled down her cheek, but her eyes were glazed, and she was not weeping.

"I understand that." She put her arm around Jackie. "It's very hard to talk about such an appalling experience, but if you report it now there is a good chance that the police will catch them."

"What good will that do?" Jackie snapped back angrily. "Will that give Mike his life back? Will it give me back my dignity, my self-respect? Will it put things back the way they were a few hours ago? Will it convince my mother that I didn't bring this on myself?"

"No, perhaps not but...."

"Then what does it matter?" Jackie's voice trembled with desperation and despair.

The nurse said nothing, for she knew not how to answer such a question. Jackie got up, and strolled towards the door.

"Remember your promise." Jackie turned in the doorway. "Tell no-one; not a living sole. Especially not my mother. She would never understand."

"I promise." The nurse answered dejectedly.

"Good." Jackie turned her back, and left.

CHAPTER SEVEN

I do not recall the moment that actually I regained consciousness, or even know how full consciousness could really be described under such circumstances.

Following an eight hour operation to rebuild my jaw, cheek and eye socket, I was given powerful pain-killing drugs which caused me to reside in a hazy world of hallucinations and dreams. I remained in this state for over a week, and have only vague recollections of consciousness.

I remember fighting for breath. The more I panicked, the more I gasped and needed air. I remember trying to tell the nurse that I couldn't breath, but she couldn't make out what I was trying to say. I remember the burning sensation in my chest, as I fought to draw breath before blacking out. I remember my mother being at my bedside, and I have vague recollections of my father being there, but very little else. During the second week in hospital, the level of drugs was reduced, and I began to become aware of my surroundings.

A huge Paddington Bear card with over a hundred get well wishes from Priory Hall hung above my bed, and the reality of what had happened began to sink in. My mother, who had been at my bedside for some ten days, had to return home, and as I began to regain my senses I started to feel quite alone. I desperately wanted to see Jackie. I could not recall her coming to visit me, but my recollection of the past few days was so sketchy that I didn't really know whether she had been or not.

As the days passed, I began to become more and more concerned by Jackie's failure to visit. I hoped that she did not blame me for what had happened. I also hoped that she felt no guilt at having run into me in the way that she had. It was clear that having being rammed from behind by the other car, she had been completely unable to avoid me. But where was she? Why hadn't she been to see me?

As I began to get stronger, I found ways of eating solid food, despite having my jaws wired together. A gap where some of my front teeth were missing was just big enough to pass small pieces of food. This was so much better than the liquid diet I had been on previously. My speech was also getting better. Nevertheless, the progress I was making physical did not compensate for my rising anxiety at Jackie's continued absence. In the end I could stand the waiting no longer, and decided to phone her parents from the hospital trolley phone. A brave step indeed, knowing as I did what they thought of me.

I was well prepared for a rude response, but I was not prepared for what I was about to be told. Jackie was dead: killed in a car accident. The news did not sink in at first, perhaps because of my medication, and I sat calmly in bed discussing with her grieving mother how the accident had happened.

Apparently her car had gone off the road, and straight into a stone railway bridge. The police were confused by the incident. It had occurred at a sharp double bend where the road went under the bridge. I knew the corner well, and so did Jackie. It was impossible to take the bend at more than about 30mph, and yet Jackie's car had been so badly crushed that it was estimated she was travelling at over 100mph. No other car had been involved. I knew immediately that it was no accident. She would never have been going so fast unless.......

The thought was so awful that I tried to banish it from my mind, but I knew in my heart it was true.

"You stupid f*****g girl." I screamed, and threw the telephone trolley against the wall in a rage. I felt the blood drain from me, and I started to shake.

The nurse came rushing through to see what had happened. She looked at the telephone, and the shaking wreck that was sat before her.

"What?" Was all she said.

I looked up at her. I could see the confusion on her face, and I felt so angry with her. I shouted at her to leave me alone, but she didn't. She sat down on the end of the bed, and continued looking at me.

"Is it Jackie?" She asked.

"She was here?" I asked, surprised that the nurse knew her name. "When? When I was unconscious?"

"The night you were brought in. We had a chat about what happened. Why, has she left you?"

"Oh, yes" I said with sarcasm and tears. "She's certainly done that all right. She's only gone and killed herself."

The nurse literally turned white in front of my eyes.

"Oh God." She mumbled. "I never thought she'd do that."

"Why?" I demanded. "What did she tell you?"

"She was a very disturbed girl, is all." The nurse paused sheepishly. "We talked briefly about what happened, while you were in theatre. I tried to persuade her to report it, but she wouldn't. I think she was too ashamed to tell her mother."

The nurse took hold of my hand, but I pulled it away.

"I'd like to be alone for a while." I asked quietly.

"Sure." The nurse turned to leave. "I'm so sorry. I wish I could have helped her."

I looked at the guilty looking woman stood before me. Her eyes told of the pain she felt at having been unable to sense how desperately Jackie had needed her help. I should have told the nurse that it was not her fault, but my thoughts were elsewhere.

My life had been spared and lost. I had lost my soul-mate. I wished with all my heart that I had never survived my injuries. My only desire was to be with my Jackie, wherever she now was.

CHAPTER EIGHT

I was released from hospital in November 1976, but was far from fully recovered. I was still in a lot of pain, and had constant double vision as a result of the damage to my right eye. I embarked on a long process of operation after operation to repair the damaged bone structure, but my physical injuries were as nothing compared to the emotional injuries that I had sustained. The loss of Jackie had left me devastated, and this sense of loss was not helped by the post-mortem discovery that Jackie had been pregnant at the time of her death. The stage of pregnancy indicated that conception had taken place during our reunion in Coventry.

I eventually returned to Lanchester Polytechnic to try and pick up my degree course, but being back in Coventry reminded me of the happy times I had spent there with Jackie. I fell into deep depression, and for the first time in my life, I had serious thoughts of suicide. After just two weeks back in Coventry, I gave up my degree course and returned to Wales.

I immediately found work as a laboratory assistant in a plastics factory called Bernard Wardle, near Caernarfon. The work was interesting enough, but I lived in a constant state of depression. I did not like meeting new people, and found it hard to chat openly with people that I didn't know well. The combination of disfigurement and natural shyness was a crippling combination; one that was to remain with me throughout my life.

I did not feel comfortable meeting new people. With people I knew well, I often tended to over-compensate by talking too much, or trying to promote an air of self-confidence which was not genuine. I lived with my parents and rarely went out, spending most of my spare time watching television, or working on my motorcycles. This life of solitude was punctuated by numerous surgical operations to improve my appearance, in the hope that one day I would be able to resume a "normal life".

One such operation was to graft replacement skin into my lower eyelid. It involved removing skin from behind my ear and inserting it into the lower eyelid to push it back into place. Unfortunately the surgeon failed to take into account the fact that the eyelid is made up of two skin surfaces, one outside and one inside. Inserting skin on the outside simply caused the eyelid to turn inwards, leaving all my eyelashes running against my eyeball. The discomfort of having a single eyelash in one's eye is as nothing compared to the pain of having a row of eyelashes rubbing on the eye 24 hours a day. Surgeons were unable to correct it for almost six months, largely because they were stumped as to what they could do to repair the situation, other than to cut the skin-graft out again.

Eventually another specialist came up with the idea of removing a piece of bone from my hip, and inserting it beneath the eyelid to hold everything in place. This worked well, however about a week later a huge red lump began forming beneath my eye. It grew and grew until it was larger than a marble, the skin becoming thinner and thinner, until finally it burst, releasing incredible amounts of blood and puss. It took months for this large open hole to finally heal, but eventually it did, and I had a period of almost a year without surgery.

Then one day I noticed what looked like a small spot forming beneath my eye. It gradually grew bigger and bigger until it burst, releasing what the doctor thought to be just puss. However it continued to ooze for weeks, and gradually a funnel shaped depression formed. I finally sought a second opinion, and it transpired that the sinus cavity had ruptured, requiring further surgery.

A series of operations took place over the years that followed. One such operation involved cutting the lower eyelid away, and re-stitching it in a different position. This surgery was so delicate, that the extra blood loss resulting from a general anaesthetic would have hindered the surgeon in his work. I therefore had to have the surgery performed under a local anaesthetic: whilst I was awake. If such an operation had been on my arm or my leg, I could have closed my eyes and ignored it, but as my lower eyelid was being cut away with a scalpel just millimetres from my eyeball, there was little I could do but watch.

My only socialising during this period was motorcycle racing, and the first success that I ever had was particularly memorable. I had been very ill for days leading up to the meeting, and had thought I would be unable to attend. A viral infection similar to mumps had caused all my glands to swell up badly around my throat and groin, causing considerable discomfort. Nevertheless, within hours of the meeting I felt sufficiently recovered to make the 300 mile journey to Cadwell Park, and I was rewarded with my first ever trophy.

In 1981 my parents' marriage broke down, and my mother was devastated by the loss of her husband to another woman. As if that was not hard enough to bear, she then developed cancer. This was not the first time she had suffered from this disease; she had had cancer over ten years before, and had been cured by radio-therapy and drugs, but this time the doctors were powerless to save her.

Towards the end of 1982, my mother became gradually weaker, a situation that was fed upon by her loss of will to live. As the cancer spread, she gradually lost the use of one of her arms, and I moved back home in order to help her cope. By the end of January

1983, the pain that my mother was suffering became so severe, that she asked to go into a hospice, where they would be able to control it better. Finally, on the 13th of February 1983, my mother died. It was the first time that I had actually witnessed somebody die. We had been told earlier that day that it was only a matter of hours, and all her family had gathered around her; my sister Alison with her husband Martin, myself, and even our father was there. We sat for hours watching her laboured breathing as she slept.

Eventually everybody else went through to a side room to have a cup of coffee. My mother would not have been aware of whether we were present or not: she was sleeping too deeply from the drugs that had been administered. As I sat there alone with her, watching her sleep, my thoughts were only that she would not have to suffer for much longer. And then it stopped. Her breathing had stopped. I took hold of her hand, and sat there watching her for several minutes. She looked no different now than when she had been breathing, just a few minutes before. Somehow I had expected more. The passing away of someone that I loved so much should have hit me harder, or should been more dramatic, or something. I didn't know what, just something.

Suddenly her body convulsed, as she took a huge gulp of breath. I jumped back, letting go of her hand. I was completely spooked by it, until I regained my senses. How could I be scared of her? She was still my mother.

She had taken just one breath, and was now lying motionless again. I knew she was gone, regardless of what her body was doing. I went through to where my family were sitting to let them know.

"I think she's gone." I told them calmly.

We all went back through to the bedside where she lay peacefully, and cried for the passing of this wonderful woman.

As I lay in bed at home later that evening, I tried to think back to the happy times we had spent as a family, but those memories lay behind a high wall. They were still there, and I could still see them if I tried hard enough, but the memories of my mother being eaten away by cancer, and distraught at the loss of her husband, were always the first to enter my mind. My most vivid memories of her were always of those final months, with her limp arm, and her face that told of pain and suffering. The mother I had really known was a happy cheerful woman, ever caring for her children, and loved by everyone who had known her. Not the woman which fate, in all its selfish splendour, had torn to shreds.

By now I had begun motor-racing in a Jaguar XJ saloon car, and in 1984 I took 4th place in the British Road Saloon Car Championship, around the circuits of Brands Hatch, Silverstone, Snetterton, Thruxton, Mallory Park, Cadwell Park, Oulton Park and Lydden Hill. As a result I was offered a place with Tom Walkinshaw Racing (TWR), who had been commissioned by Jaguar to win the coveted Le Mans 24 hour race.

I also became increasingly interested in wildlife and wildlife conservation, an interest which I had developed as a child, and then forgotten when I became keen on motorcycles. In 1986 I began doing voluntary work for the British Trust for Conservation Volunteers in my spare time. One such project took me to Bardsey Island, a small island off the Lleyn Peninsula in North Wales. The island was a nature reserve, and an important site for observing bird migration. Despite the fact that Bardsey lay less than a kilometre from the mainland, to reach the island required a two hour boat journey from Pwllheli. Apparently this was because the closest village did not have boats of sufficient size to take us across.

We were supposed to be on Bardsey for just a week, but had been warned to take provisions for a couple of extra days, in case rough weather prevented the boat from picking us up on time. As it turned out, we were stranded for more than two weeks, and our rations proved totally inadequate for such an extended stay. Towards the end of the second week, we had absolutely nothing left to eat except potatoes, not even any cooking oil to make chips. We had boiled potatoes for breakfast, lunch and evening meal. I never wanted to see another potato.

On the fourteenth day the weather was very calm and sunny, and we were confident of being collected by the boat at long last. We went to the top of the mountain to make contact using the short-wave radio, to ask what time we were to be collected. To our dismay, we were told that the window of calm weather was too short for the 4 hour round trip from Pwllheli. We sat on top of the mountain with rumbling stomachs, admiring the spectacular views of the mainland so close by, wondering if we would ever get home. As if to rub salt into our wounds, we watched a group of scouts paddle out from the mainland, around our island, and back to the mainland in canoes! We were not amused.

A couple of days later we were finally picked up by the boat, and taken back to Pwllheli where we pigged ourselves on pie and chips, and a mountain of cream cakes. It was not such a happy homecoming for me however, since I was greeted by the news that my grandmother had died.

Despite the ordeal of Bardsey Island I continued to work for BTCV, and eventually became involved in Baseline Survey work. This work immediately grabbed my interest, and I began conducting Coastline Surveys along the Menai Straits for the Nature Conservancy Council. I really enjoyed the work, and decided to develop my career in this direction.

In order to establish a career in Biological Surveying, it was important to become professionally qualified, and to that end I began doing a degree course through the Open University. Due to the high demand of people wishing to enrol on the Science Foundation Course, all the places had been taken for that year. This left me with a choice of delaying the start of my studies for another year, or enrolling on the second level course first.

I opted to take Biology as my second level course, in the belief that I had sufficient background knowledge of Biology to cope without having done the foundation course. This proved to be the case initially, but I ran into real trouble when I got onto the Biochemistry section. The Foundation Course provides the necessary background education that is required for second level courses, and I was completely stuck without this background knowledge of biochemistry.

It seemed as though I would be unable to continue, but not wishing to give up without a fight, I went to the local library and took out several textbooks on basic Chemistry and Biochemistry. I read them through until I understood the principals involved, and then returned to my Biology course work. I was now able to make sense of the course material, but I was well behind schedule. With lots of late nights, and sympathetic tutors prepared to accept late assignments, I gradually managed to claw back the lost time. Amazingly I passed my second level Biology course with a score of 86% (Grade One).

I enrolled on the Open University Science Foundation Course in 1989, but soon afterwards I heard of a new post-graduate Biological Surveying course that was starting at Otley College. I knew that this was the course for me, and immediately applied. My only concern was that being a post-graduate course, I would not be accepted without having first completed my degree. As it turned out my Baseline Surveying work for the Nature Conservancy Council was accepted in place of a degree, and I began the course in September 1989.

I did not wish to drop out of my Open University degree course, so I decided to do both courses together. Normally such a work load would have been impossible, but my scientific background gave me enough knowledge to make the Science Foundation course easy, so I coped. I passed my Biological Surveying and Conservation Management courses with Distinction in July 1990, and was offered work by the US Government, conducting research work for the Hawaii Volcanoes National Park Service.

On 25th June 1991 I flew out of Gatwick, destined for Hawaii. About ten minutes after take-off we were told that we were returning to Gatwick due to engine problems. A second announcement told us that because we had too much weight of fuel onboard for landing, that we were going to fly around for half an hour dumping fuel.

The passengers seated in front of me immediately began discussing how unusual that was, and began speculating that it was more probable that there was a bomb onboard. They quickly worked themselves up into a right panic, and began to make surrounding passengers nervous. I was never very convinced by the bomb theory, but I was very glad to get off the plane at Gatwick, just in case.

Several hours later we got underway again, and after a short sleep I began to look out of the window. For some considerable time I had seen only ocean, but then I began to notice tiny white spots against the background of blue. The white spots became larger and more abundant, and I realised that they were icebergs. Suddenly a frozen coastline came into view, and as we flew over it I could see huge glaciers winding their way up snow-covered valleys. Further inland the valleys became increasingly covered in snow, until eventually only the mountain peaks protruded above the snowy blanket.

Gradually less and less peaks became visible until there was little to see except the smooth white blanket of snow. A short while later peaks began to appear again, and became more and more abundant. Glaciated valleys began appearing, and then we were flying back across another frozen coastline. We had flown over the very heart of Greenland, and had undoubtedly seen the peaks of mountains that no man had ever set foot on. I gazed in awe as the little white dots floating in the ocean below slowly dwindled away.

A little while later we flew over the seemingly endless labyrinth of islands and channels of New Foundland. Thousands upon thousands of islands with barely a house or a road to be seen. After changing planes at Dallas, the second leg of our journey took us across the Rocky Mountains range, another vast empty wilderness with very few roads or settlements. I began to realise just how wild and unpopulated North America was.

I arrived the following day in sunny Honolulu. I was immediately struck by the bright colours everywhere. All around there were beautiful, brightly coloured birds and flowers, and even the people were dressed in brightly coloured clothes. The air was warm, and the sun shone brightly. All around there were palm trees, and despite the hustle and bustle of the city, there was an underlying sense of peace and tranquillity.

From Honolulu I flew to Hilo on the Big Island of Hawaii, from which the archipelago takes its name. I was met by two Americans, Mathew and Eric, who took me to the National Park Headquarters which was to be my home for the next few months. I settled myself in, and then went to bed to catch up on some much needed sleep.

The following day I met the National Park Service staff, and was given a briefing as to what the work would entail, and how the organisation operated. I then went to do some sight-seeing. A few hundred yards from the headquarters there was a hotel. I entered through the foyer, and wandered out onto the veranda to the rear. I gazed in amazement at the sight that befell my eyes.

In front of me lay a giant volcanic crater some three kilometres across, with a jet black crust of hardened lava at its base, and sheer walls of luxurious hanging vegetation. Steam billowed out of cracks in the fissured crust of lava, and the air held a scent of sulphur. It was as though I had stepped back in time to a prehistoric world. All that was lacking were the dinosaurs.

The following day we were off on turtle patrol. Loaded up with a backpack that contained everything I needed for 5 days, I set off on the hike to Apua Point behind Eric and Mathew. The route took us along the coastline, over solidified black lava that had flowed down from Mauna Loa a few years before. The surface was shiny and brittle like glass. The sun's rays beat down upon us, heating up the lava underfoot, and making the hike hard and tiring. We stopped half way, near an abandoned corral built from blocks of lava, and took some much needed water.

Two hours later we reached our destination, and set up camp. A simple tubular frame with a tarpaulin over it would be home for the duration. It was too hot for any other kind of tent. Apua Point was a small cobble beach, and was one of just three known nesting sites for the Hawaiian Hawksbill Turtle. The Hawksbill had once been numerous around Hawaii, but hotels built on breeding sites, slaughter for its shell to make tortoiseshell, and entanglement in fishing nets, had brought the Hawksbill Turtle to the very brink of extinction in Hawaii.

Our job was to take turns at patrolling the beach throughout the night searching for female turtles coming ashore to lay eggs. If we spotted one, we were to observe her egg-laying activities, record the location of any eggs that she laid, and mark her with metal flipper tags. I soon discovered that the Hawksbill Rescue Programme was so new that nobody had actually seen one come ashore yet. Their presence at the nesting sites was known only from flipper tracks left on the beach.

After several nights of patrolling the beach we had seen nothing, but the week had by no means been wasted. Right in front of our camp site was a wonderful coral reef, which was a haven for marine life. There was no need for scuba diving, just a snorkel and mask was all that was needed to enter this wonderland. Apart from the brightly coloured corals themselves, there was a variety of interesting fish, from Moray Eels to Angel Fish.

Perhaps the most bizarre experience was found deep inside the numerous fissures that one found inland. The fissures had been formed by earthquakes, and were very deep and narrow: so deep that they went down to below the ground water table. When we wanted to cool off, we could climb down inside these cracks and enter the cool freshwater. This was so much more refreshing than bathing in salt-water.

Within a minute or two of entering the water we would feel things crawling over our skin. They were freshwater shrimps which lived nowhere else on earth except in these freshwater cracks. The shrimps would crawl all over us picking off little bits of dead skin. The small ones tickled, but the larger ones could be up to about 10cm long, and they hurt, especially when they tried to pinch pieces of skin from between our toes.

Back at Park Headquarters, I was considered to be fully trained after one week in the field. It wasn't much of a background, but since nobody had yet laid eyes on one of the elusive turtles, it was all there was. A few days later I was sent back to Apua Point with a new assistant called Tamara.

Upon arrival back at Apua Point we noticed fresh turtle tracks across some of the sandy areas of the beach, further evidence that this was indeed an active nesting site. I took the first watch from 8pm until midnight.

We had been instructed not to use flashlights for fear of scaring away the turtles, so it was very difficult to see much in the dark. I had soon discovered that the best way to look for turtles was to sit or lie in the centre of the beach, so that the cobbles of the beach were highlighted against the white surf. After about an hour, it occurred to me that a large boulder that I had been looking at for some time was getting larger. And it was moving.

I tried using the binoculars to get a better view, and sure enough it was a turtle. I watched as she slowly laboured her way up over the cobbles towards me. She seemed to be heading straight towards me, but I didn't want to move for fear of scaring her away. I decided that it was probably best to remain still, and allow her to pass by me of her own accord. Eventually she came and stopped right in front of me. I could have reached out and touched her, but I didn't. She was a magnificent creature, with a total length of well over a metre.

Eventually she turned slightly and pushed past the side of me, bashing my leg with her flailing flippers as she did so. She finally reached the strip of sand at the back of the beach where the vegetation was, and began digging a pit for her eggs. I rushed back to get Tamara and the tagging equipment, before returning once more to watch the proceedings. We watched her dig two pits during the course of two hours, but for whatever reason she abandoned both pits without laying.

Hawksbill Turtles often dig several 'false nests' before finding one which has just the right conditions for laying. Since the temperature of the nest determines the sex of the hatchlings, factors such as moisture content and grain size must be just right for her to lay. As she began making her way back over the cobbles again towards the ocean, it was apparent that she had abandoned her nesting attempt for the night.

We had been instructed to observe the nesting attempt through to its conclusion without disturbance. Once she began heading back to sea however, we were to measure her length and tag her front flippers with metal tags for identification. This was important. It was known that turtles could lay several clutches during a season, so without marking each turtle it would have been impossible to know how many turtles were nesting at each site.

We had been given instructions as to how to fit the tag through the loose skin close to the arm-pit of the front flipper, but despite the theory, nobody had ever tagged a Hawaiian Hawksbill before, so we were very much on our own.

I began by grabbing hold of the back of the turtle's shell to stop her leaving, but this had no effect whatsoever. The turtle was so powerful that it dragged me along the beach with ease. Tamara went round in front to help me stop it, but it bulldozed past her with disdain. Finally I whisked off my shirt and placed it over the turtles head and eyes. Amazingly she stopped. It seemed that as long as we held the shirt firmly over her head and eyes, she remained still.

Tamara took over holding my shirt over the eyes, whilst I took out the tagging pliers and loaded them with a metal identification tag. I found the correct spot at the back of the front flipper, and squeezed the pliers together, pushing the tag through the fleshy part of the flipper. It worked perfectly, and the turtle barely moved. I repeated the process with the other front flipper.

The next task was to measure the size of the carapace (shell), and to do this we had a giant set of callipers. At this point Tamara let go of the turtles head, and it began lumbering forward once more. This was not a problem, since at the speed that she was travelling I could still take my measurements with ease. Tamara grabbed her camera, and began taking photographs as I took the measurements.

Finally we stood back and watched the turtle slowly enter the surf and swim away. I felt very satisfied with a job well done, and congratulated Tamara on her excellent assistance. I felt slight concern at the disturbance caused by fitting the tags, but reminded myself that it was an essential procedure if these ancient creatures were to be saved from extinction. As it turned out, the value of fitting the tags was to prove its worth far more rapidly than we could have imagined.

As soon as the Headquarters staff turned in for work the following morning, I called my boss, Andy Kikuta, on the radio to give him the news. I was incredibly excited at having tagged the first ever Hawaiian Hawksbill Turtle, and gave Andy a twenty minute account of the events. I was quite sure that he would share my excitement, but he didn't.

"Well that's good." He replied in a rather apathetic tone. "but Michael, in future could you make your transmissions just a little shorter. This radio frequency is used by the whole Park."

What the heck. So what if every Park Ranger, Tourist Guide and Estate Worker within a fifty kilometre radius had had to stop work to listen to my turtle tagging report. This was important. Well, perhaps he did have a point.

The very next evening Tamara was on watch when a turtle came ashore again. We were immediately able to determine that this was indeed "our" turtle back to try again. She was still wearing her shiny metal flipper tags from the previous night. She dug two more pits over a period of three hours, but again abandoned them both. Once again she returned to the ocean without laying.

The fact that she had returned again so soon after being tagged was very gratifying. It demonstrated that turtles were not easily put off by the experience of being tagged and measured. Indeed, despite the experience, she had not shown the least bit of concern at our presence. On several occasions she had pushed right past us in her search for a suitable nest site. I was sorry to see her return to the ocean after another fruitless night's toil, but I had no doubt that she would return to try again.

Indeed she did, but as the season progressed our tagging programme revealed that the population of turtles was very much smaller than anybody had expected. Rather than having several turtles nesting at each of the sites, as had been supposed, there were in fact just one or two nesting females using each of the sites. The fact that each female visited several times before successfully laying, and laid several clutches during a season, had made it appear as though there were far more turtles than was actually the case. Our turtle monitoring also dispelled another myth.

It had been previously supposed that introduced mongoose and rats were responsible for digging up turtle nests in order to eat the eggs. During the previous season several large pits had been found where the nests had been dug up and the eggs eaten. Nevertheless, turtle eggs were usually buried more than half a metre below the sand, and it was hard to imagine how such small animals could have dug such large pits to get at the eggs.

One night I was at Apua Point with Tamara, observing another turtle searching for a place to lay her eggs. The turtle spent about twenty minutes investigating suitable sites along the edge of the vegetation, before choosing a spot to start digging. After about thirty minutes of digging, the pit was starting to get quite large, and we had our fingers crossed that she would lay. As her flippers flicked the sand behind her I noticed an egg. To begin with I was confused by what I saw, since she had clearly not got into a laying position, and was still in the process of digging. I carefully used my torch to look into the hole, and saw a number of eggs half buried in the sand. I realised that she was in fact digging in the spot where she had laid eggs the month before.

I did what seemed the only sensible thing to do, and pulled her out of the pit by the carapace (shell). She began wandering off along the edge of the vegetation, and we replaced the eggs and covered them over with sand again. Even if we had disturbed her to the point where she abandoned digging for the night, it was still better than allowing her to destroy a complete nest that had already been laid. In actual fact she choose another spot to dig, and carried on as if nothing had happened.

This had solved the riddle of egg predation. Since Apua Point had such a small area of sand where laying could take place, the turtles were digging where nests had previously been laid. When these pits were then abandoned without laying, the eggs dug up were left scattered around the pit, where mongoose and rats would find and eat them. This had made it appear as if the mongoose and rats were capable of excavating nests, which was very doubtful. As for the eggs, even if they had not been eaten, they would have been baked by the sun without a sufficient covering of sand.

By now our turtle monitoring programme was moving into its second phase, as some of the nests neared the point of hatching. Under normal circumstances this would have been an observational exercise only, but Apua Point was a death-trap for hatchlings, quite literally.

Some years before, a major earthquake had caused the surrounding area of coastline to sink, changing the beach structure at Apua. What had once been a small sandy bay had now become a cobble beach with just a thin strip of sand at the top against the vegetation. This was the area that the turtles used for nesting, drawn back to their birthplace by instinct. The large females were able to crawl over the cobbles without too much difficulty, but for the tiny hatchlings it was a very different story.

Hatchlings emerged under cover of darkness, and were drawn towards the ocean by the lighter horizon. Each nest held about a hundred and seventy eggs, and the hatchlings would emerge from the sand in groups, and head towards the sea like an army of clockwork toys. Few got more than a few metres. One by one they fell into the gaps amongst the large cobbles and became trapped. With no escape, they were doomed to be baked to death when the sun reached its peak the following day.

Our job was to patrol the beach throughout the night, searching for nests that were hatching. This was not too difficult since we had previously documented where each of the nests were, and when they had been laid. We knew to within a few days when each particular nest was due to hatch. Once the hatchlings emerged, we would put them into buckets, and carry them down to the waters edge to be released. This was easier said than done with so many hatchlings emerging together. The problem was exacerbated by the fact that many hatchlings would be carried back onto the beach by the surf, and become trapped in the cobbles again.

Without our efforts all the hatchlings would have perished. We never found any that had made it more than half way across the cobbles on their own. We spent hours hunting through the cobbles to make sure that all the hatchlings had got beyond the surf and into the open ocean. I was spurred on by the thought that some of the hatchlings that I had saved might one day return to this beach, probably long after I had departed from this world.

Being something of a newcomer to marine turtle conservation, I had generally accepted what I had been told, and followed my instructions to the letter. Nevertheless, it became increasingly apparent to me that it would be much easier to put some kind of enclosure around the nest prior to hatching. By doing so we would merely need to monitor the enclosures, and when the nests did hatch, we would not need to search for the hatchlings amongst the cobbles.

I discussed my idea with Andy, and he agreed, so I hiked out to Apua Point with a roll of chicken wire, and made large circular enclosures to put around each nest. It worked a treat. The hatchlings could now be collected without the risk of becoming lost in the cobbles.

Another idea that I discussed with Andy, was the method of release. It had been my understanding that turtles returned to their birthplace to lay, because the beach was somehow imprinted on them at birth. The actual mechanism of imprinting was unknown, and it occurred to me that by placing hatchlings directly into the water, we may be interfering with this mechanism.

I therefore suggested that we took the hatchlings a hundred metres along the beach to a small section that was free of cobbles, and allowed them to make their own way to the sea from there. After consultation with George Balazs, a local marine biologist, Andy agreed that we should make the change.

We also began digging up nests a few days after hatching. Invariably there were a few hatchlings that had been unable to escape from the nest, and which would otherwise have perished. This did not mean that these hatchlings were weaklings, they had simply been stuck in the middle of surrounding egg shells, and had no means of escape.

By the end of the season, we had released almost a thousand hatchlings from Apua Point, all of which would otherwise have perished on the cobbles. From the tagging programme we were able to estimate that the total Hawaiian Hawksbill population was no more than twenty mature females. This was the very brink of extinction. If this remarkable animal was to endure, then every single hatchling counted.

With the work on turtles now completed for the year, I went on to help with the Hawaiian Geese, also known as Nenes. Nenes are only found in Hawaii, and they had been rescued from the very brink of extinction during the 1950s when the population had dropped to just 34 birds. Since then numbers had been increased to a few hundred by captive breeding, but the population still seemed unable to sustain itself in the wild. The problem was that virtually all the chicks died within a few days of hatching. It was supposed that introduced mongoose killed the goslings, but without actually observing what was happening to the goslings, it was impossible to say for certain. Our job was to observe the goslings, and try to ascertain what was happening to them.

Unlike the turtle programme, the Nene programme had been running for years, and each year the same procedure was used. Firstly we searched for Nenes that had nests, and once we located a nest with eggs, we attached a radio transmitter to one of the adults. The goslings abandon the nest immediately after hatching, and follow the adults to areas of good feeding. By attaching a radio transmitter to one of the adults, we were able to locate the family group whenever we wanted to, in order to monitor their progress.

Unfortunately Howard, the project leader, was not in favour of prolonged observations of any particular family group. He much preferred daily checks on each of the family groups, but this meant that only a few minutes were spent with each family. Most of each day was spent walking around searching for the family groups. This approach did not reveal much information, since we never observed why the goslings were disappearing. One day we might observe a family with three goslings, and the following day there would be only two. Within two or three weeks of hatching, invariable the goslings were all lost, but without having observed them disappearing we were none the wiser as to why.

The work was further hampered by the fact that the project was run during office hours only. Work finished at 5pm each day, and no work was done at weekends. Hardly surprising that many years of monitoring had revealed virtually nothing. Unlike the turtle programme, the Nene programme had a very rigid management regime, and suggested improvements were not welcome.

During my work on the Nene programme I struck up a friendship with a particularly tame Nene, called NA. He was called NA simply because of his leg band which read "NA". Whenever I was out searching for Nenes I would very often come across NA, and he would come across to see what I was doing. It was a friendship that I nurtured, sharing my lunch with him, and using his friendship to gain the trust of other Nene's that I wished to capture for banding or study.

In 1992 Andy Kikuta left, and the turtle monitoring programme was placed under the control of Larry Katahira, who had very different views. Larry had a much more autocratic style of management than Andy. Both had very little experience of actually carrying out fieldwork, but Andy had always been prepared to listen to suggestions given by those who did have the experience. Larry was not.

In October 1992, two German girls called Anja and Heidrun came to work on the Turtle Programme. After being given the usual training, they were sent out to Apua Point to watch for emerging hatchlings. A few days later I was sent out on my own to take over from them, and was horrified by what I saw.

Walking along the beach I found a dead hatchling on the cobbles, and then another, and then another. The more I looked, the more I found. In total I recovered over 50 dead hatchlings, and 3 live ones which were very weak. The netting enclosures that I had made the previous year were still in use, but they had put them in the wrong spot.

Apparently Anja and Heidrun had decided to spend the day hiking down the coast, and had not bothered to check the beach prior to leaving. There was always a risk that hatchlings might be missed during darkness, and for this reason an early morning check of the beach was a priority. Provided hatchlings were discovered before the sun became too strong, they could still be rescued. It was unclear whether this tragedy had resulted from poor training or negligence, but it had certainly been avoidable.

No more hatchlings emerged from the nest, so I requested permission to dig up the nest to release the remaining hatchlings trapped amongst the egg shells. To my dismay Larry refused permission for me to do so. He told me that our job was to monitor only, and not to interfere with natural processes. Being completely alone on an isolated beach, I dug up the nest anyway, and released 25 healthy hatchlings that were trapped amongst the egg shells. These were the only hatchlings to have survived out of the entire nest of 174 eggs. I re-buried the nest again so that other workers would not realise that I had excavated it.

I had managed to save 25 hatchlings from this nest, but the underlying problem was that other field-workers were being instructed not to excavate the nests. This inevitably led to the unnecessary loss of hatchlings that were vital to the Hawksbill's survival in the islands. At the end of the season, Larry sent out a team to excavate all the season's nests to count the number of eggs that had hatched. In addition to the empty egg shells, they also discovered hundreds of dead hatchlings that could have been so easily saved. A tragic waste.

Larry was completely unconcerned by this unnecessary loss, but his superior Dan Taylor was not, and took disciplinary action against Larry. So much of what we learnt during the first season with Andy had been lost, simply because of a change of management. It will always remain my view that when a population is on the very brink of extinction, it is too late to apply a non-intervention policy. Unless the human factors which had brought about the decline were counteracted, then the outcome was inevitable. For the few remaining Hawaiian Hawksbill Turtles, time had all but expired.

In 1993 I left Hawaii to take up employment as Conservation Officer for the Falkland Islands, a tiny island off the coast of Argentina. My work in Hawaii had barely equipped me for the challenges which lay ahead.

PART 2: The Falklands Regime

*How to overcome an organisation whose role stands
in the way of greed?
Secure a governing role within that organisation, and
destroy it from within.
How to overcome an individual whose honesty stands
in the way of greed?
Discredit him with false claims of dishonesty, until the
truth becomes obscured.*

CHAPTER NINE

The very first time that man set foot on the Falkland Islands is unknown. The first recorded settling of the Falklands took place in 1764, but it is certain that humans had visited long before, and probably settled for a while. Evidence of this can be found in the history of the Falklands' fauna.

Geologically the Falkland Islands have never been part of South America. Geological evidence shows that the Falklands actually broke away from the African continent millions of years ago, before the evolution of mammals and birds, and moved towards South America as a result of continental drift. As such, the Falklands have never been in contact with continental mammals and birds, which evolved after the Falklands became isolated. Those species present in the Falklands prior to human settlement must have travelled there by wind or sea.

It is well known that virgin islands which sprout up from the ocean floor through volcanic activity can become colonised by species which are blown across by storms, or which drift across on ocean currents. Hawaii and the Galapagos Islands are two well known examples. Such islands demonstrate a hierarchy of colonisation.

The first to colonise are marine species, which arrive on the beaches as free swimming individuals or drifters on ocean currents. Everything from seaweeds and crabs, to turtles and seals can quickly colonise new lands. Hawaii is the world's most remote example of island colonisation, lying alone in the centre of the Pacific Ocean between the continents of America and Asia, and yet marine species all reached Hawaii early in its history. Indeed these marine species come and go with such ease that they continue to mix with populations in other parts of the world, preventing the formation of new species. The turtles found in Hawaii are the same species found throughout the equatorial regions of the world, as are the seaweeds, crabs and fish.

Species found on dry land naturally find it harder to reach remote islands, with plants, birds and insects being the first to arrive, carried by their own power of flight, or as passive riders of the wind. Seeds and insects often use the wind to disperse over large areas, and over thousands of years freak conditions will blow a few of them thousands of miles across oceans to colonise distant lands. Hawaii lies over two thousand miles from the nearest continent, and yet plants, birds and insects were blown onto this virgin land, where they flourished. Because their crossing was such an improbable event, they were cut off from the genetic pool from which they came, and evolved to form new species unique to Hawaii.

Animals which cannot be carried by the wind rely on floating to distant islands, and even allowing for freak occurrences, some animals cannot make such a crossing. No land mammals had ever colonised Hawaii or the Galapagos islands until man introduced them. Indeed the only way for land mammals to colonise remote islands would be for a pregnant female to drift across on ocean currents, but the high energy requirement of warm-blooded mammals would lead to their starvation long before they could drift so far.

However cold-blooded reptiles, which have a much lower energy requirement, did make it to the Galapagos Islands carried by ocean currents. Tortoises have the ability to float on their backs if they fall into water, and being cold-blooded they are able to survive low body temperatures and long periods without food, enabling them to survive the journey drifting across the ocean. Being a reptile, a single female tortoise washed up on a beach can colonise new lands simply by laying eggs.

Tortoises and iguanas both reached the Galapagos Islands, and being cut off from their genetic pool, formed new species. However no reptiles ever reached the Falklands. The Falklands is nearer to the continental mainland than either Hawaii or the Galapagos Islands, but the oceanic crossing is very different. The equatorial Pacific currents around the Galapagos Islands are warm, in stark contrast to the cold South Atlantic currents around the Falklands. Even reptiles could not survive the cold sea temperatures of a southern ocean crossing from South America to the Falklands.

No reptiles or amphibians ever reached the Falklands, and yet the Falklands had the Warrah. The Warrah was a fox unique to the Falklands. Very different from its South American counterparts, it had clearly lived in the Falklands for a very long time. And yet is it likely that against the evidence from every other virgin island on earth, a pregnant female fox drifted across from South America, surviving the freezing ocean journey to spawn a new species?

It takes two days for a powered vessel to make the crossing. Ocean currents do not run in the direction of travel, so it would require strong winds to move debris across from South America to the Falklands. Such a crossing would take weeks, and the survival time for a warm-blooded animal in these freezing waters would be minutes, certainly not days or weeks. The ancestor of the Warrah could not have just drifted across. With no land bridge ever having existed, the only explanation is that the Warrah was descended from foxes that had been brought across by early human visitors to the Falklands, just like the land mammals now found in Hawaii and the Galapagos Islands.

Whoever these early visitors to the Falklands were has never been discovered. The most likely source would be Tierra del Fuego or Patagonia, but that is just speculation. Their boats, clothes and tools, made of wood and hide, would not have been easily preserved. Other than the presence of the Warrah, there is no other evidence of their visit to the Falklands. When man settled the Falklands in the 18th century, he quickly drove the Warrah to extinction.

The Falklands has always been a hard place to make a living. Wind-swept and open, the weather can be very inhospitable to human settlers, and yet the wildlife that made its way to the Falklands thrived. Three hundred species of plants, some sixty species of birds, and an unknown number of invertebrates adapted to the Falklands climate. Not rich in species diversity, the Falklands was immensely rich in quantity. With few predators, and a coastline that offered a surplus of breeding sites, huge seabird populations were controlled only by food available. And food was plentiful. Millions upon millions of penguins thrived on the rich feeding grounds of the Patagonian Shelf, which made the Falklands a paradise for seabirds and marine mammals. This abundant wildlife was to become an important economic resource for human visitors and settlers.

Prior to the proliferation of electric lighting during the twentieth century, lighting was mostly by oil lamp, and prior to the development of oil and gas reserves, the oil used for lighting came from whales and seals. Whaling was big business, and the waters around the Falklands was a favoured hunting ground. Seals and sealions were also killed for their skins and oil, and even penguins were slaughtered for the small amount of oil they contained. Live penguins were thrown onto open fires so that their body fat fuelled the fires, which in turn heated giant cauldrons which melted down the seal carcasses into blubber and oil.

Whales and seals reproduce slowly, and the slaughter of so many caused populations to collapse. But penguins can reproduce rapidly if food is abundant. Despite the huge numbers of penguins killed by sealers and whalers, penguin populations remained high, the high adult mortality being compensated by rapid reproduction made possible through an abundance of fish and squid.

Many vessels visited the Falklands during the 16th and 17th centuries, harvesting seals and penguins, and collecting eggs and fowl, but the first documented colonisation of the Falklands was by the French. On 31st January 1764, a young French officer, Luis Antoine Bouganville, landed on the islands and began to build a settlement in the north-east corner of East Falkland. Cape Bouganville still bears his name. On 5th April 1764, Bouganville claimed the archipelago in the name of King Luis XV of France and named the islands 'Les Malouines'.

King Charles III of Spain immediately protested to the French government for what he saw as an incursion into Spanish territory in the South Atlantic under the terms of the 1713 Utrecht Treaty and the Families Pact of 1761, and on 1st April 1767, France handed the colony over to Spain, who occupied and administered the Falklands for the next 45 years.

In 1766 a British settlement was established at Port Egmont on Saunders Island. The Spanish authorities in Buenos Aires ordered the expulsion of the British settlers, and this was carried out in June 1770. A year later, British settlers return to Port Egmont and remained there until 1774, when they were again forced to leave.

In February 1811, the Spanish settlers on the Falklands were withdrawn to reinforce Spanish troops exiled in Uruguay, in a final attempt to resist the independence movement of Buenos Aires. After three years of battles the Spanish forces were finally defeated in Montevideo on 20th June 1814. Two years later, at the Tucumán Congress on 9th July 1816, the United Provinces of the River Plate (later to become Argentina) formally declared independence from Spain. They declared possession of the Falklands in 1820, and resettled at Port Louis in 1833, 22 years after the Spanish had left. By this time the British had also settled the islands, and set up British administration of the islands, a situation which was to lead to a long-standing dispute with Argentina over sovereignty.

During the nineteenth century, the Falkland Islands developed an unsavoury reputation for swindling innocent seafarers seeking repair work for damaged ships. Trade between Europe and the Pacific coasts of the Americas was a booming business, especially following the North American gold-rush of the 1800s, and the only shipping route for this trade meant rounding Cape Horn. Cape Horn is notorious for its fierce storms, and those ships which survived the journey often sustained damage.

The Falklands' close proximity to Cape Horn meant that ships which became damaged rounding the Horn would limp to Port Stanley in the hope of repair. Whilst the Falklands did hold a well skilled work-force capable of undertaking such repairs, they were more intent on stranding vessels in the Falklands so that they could lay claim to the ships' valuable cargo and timber.

Through outrageous quotes for repair, and down right sabotage, many ships were written off as economically beyond repair, leaving ship owners and crew to seek payment through insurers, whilst Port Stanley acquired timber and a variety of cargo that was going nowhere without a vessel. Many of the wrecks around Stanley Harbour were acquired in just such a manner, making useful warehouses for the windfall of goods left stranded, and many of the oldest buildings in Stanley are built from ships' timber.

With the discovery of the Straits of Magellan, and the building of lighthouses along its length in the early 1900s, ships no longer needed to round Cape Horn. The trade in damaged ships declined, and the Venus Fly-trap of the shipping world turned to other business.

Sheep-farming has been the backbone of the Falklands' economy since early settlement, and throughout most of the twentieth century this was the Falklands' main income. Sheep-farming is a hard way to make a living, especially in the harsh Falklands climate. Such hard graft for an honest wage did not suit the free-loaders and charlatans of the day, and their departure moulded the character of the true Falkland Islander - down to earth, hard working, friendly and above all honest. These qualities still exist today, but have become oppressed by the return of the charlatans seeking easy money from commercial fishing and oil exploration.

In 1982 the long-standing dispute with Argentina boiled over into war, with Argentina taking the islands by force on 2nd April 1982. Britain responded by sending a military fleet which liberated the islands on 14th June 1982 at the cost of many hundreds of lives. The Argentine soldiers gave their lives believing that they were liberating the islands. They had been told that they would be welcomed by the oppressed islanders, who would greet them with cheers and flowers. This was a lie. They were greeted with spitting and hatred by a population who saw them as invaders. The British soldiers gave their lives believing they were upholding democracy; the right for Falkland Islanders to live free from tyranny and oppression, which as history has since shown, was also a lie.

Prior to the 1982 war the Falklands was a thorn in the side of the British government, one which they were seeking diplomatic means to extract. Eight thousand miles away, and an unwelcome drain on the British economy, the two thousand inhabitants of the Falklands meant little to Britain. Indeed, apart from the islanders themselves, it was only Argentina that really wanted the Falklands. Had Argentina shown a moderate degree of patience, they would have eventually gained ownership of the islands by diplomatic means. However the faltering Argentine government of the time needed a quick fix for its disastrous economic policies, and thought that the popularity of taking the Falklands by force would do the trick.

The invasion of the Falklands did lift the Argentine government on a wave of public support, but this popularity was short lived, as an equally determined

British Prime Minister, Margaret Thatcher, dug her heels in, and vowed to re-take the islands. Whilst letting the Falklands gradually slip away through diplomacy was acceptable, having Argentina take a piece of British Territory by force was not. Failure to reclaim the Falklands from a Latin American dictator would have meant the end of Britain's reputation as a major world power, and Margaret Thatcher was determined to ensure that this would not happen under her reign.

In just a little over 2 months the Argentine forces had surrendered, 266 British and 649 Argentines lay dead, and Britain had won back a sheep-farming outpost that they had been trying to get rid of for years. Politicians in Whitehall decided that having gone to so much trouble winning back the Falklands, that they had better do something with it. After years of neglect the British government finally looked into ways of rejuvenating the Falklands economy, and came up with a very simple plan.

During the 1970s increasingly large numbers of fishing vessels had been fishing around the Falklands, many from countries which by now had depleted their own fish stocks through over-fishing. In conjunction with representatives of the Falklands community, it was decided in a series of secret talks that a 300 kilometre control zone would be established around the Falklands, and that in future any vessels wishing to fish in these waters would have to pay a large fee. All that was needed was a licensing system, and people to sell the licences.

With the smell of money in the air, and the realisation that more fingers in the pie meant less pie, it did not take long for certain people involved in these secret talks to claim a head-start in ensuring their slice of the wealth. Giving up secure employment to set up fishing companies appeared like madness to other Falkland Islanders, until the secret plan was revealed. Much of the division of wealth which exists in the Falklands today stems from these shrewd, if not dishonest, dealings. In Britain such insider-trading would be illegal, but in the Falklands politics and making money go hand in hand.

With fishing vessels paying hundreds of thousands of pounds each for licences, the money started pouring in - more money than the select few knew what to do with. Many set up auxiliary companies which spread their wealth into a variety of other enterprises, helping to disguise the true source of their millions. Within a couple of years the Falkland Islands had turned from poverty, to an annual income of over £20,000 (US$30,000) for every man, woman and child. But that money was never distributed evenly amongst the population. Those who had been seated at the table of plenty by British government colleagues claimed the majority of the private wealth, whilst the rest of the population were forced to seek their share of the wealth through the many lucrative government jobs.

Of course the best paid jobs always went to friends of friends, with success passing down through families and the Old Boys Network. Many beneficiaries were living overseas, brought in on contracts paying hefty salaries, complete with housing, trips abroad and the many other comforts to which they had never been accustomed. Many such contract officers were not even needed, and commenced their appointment by re-structuring the smooth operation of government to make themselves indispensable. Change a simple system which works, for something horrendously complicated, and all of a sudden nobody can do without the new people who run the system.

This was the hay-day of the Falklands economy. A time to build a modern new school and hospital, which would be the envy of any British town. A time to build an EEC standard abattoir to process a handful of sheep, a road system to link every remote farm, and a new house for the Governor. A time to introduce charges for children wanting to use the football field, and strict laws to control who does and doesn't have the right to share the wealth. A time to appoint two supervisors to every worker, to establish a scheme giving free holidays to all 'qualifying' citizens, and for sending government officials to exotic locations on 'fact-finding' missions. One such mission resulted in Chief Executive Andrew Gurr proposing the construction of a Cotswold village in a remote sheep-farming outpost in south Falkland!

But this surplus of wealth came with a hidden price tag. With huge amounts of fish and squid being removed from the waters around the Falklands, it was perhaps not surprising that seabirds and seals which relied on the same fish and squid for food began declining. But in 1993 nobody had ever done a wildlife census to realise what was happening. Enter the bearer of bad tidings - a messenger, who as is often the case, was about to be shot for his efforts.

CHAPTER TEN

I arrived in the Falklands in October 1993 to take up the post of Conservation Officer for Falklands Conservation, a government funded conservation organisation. I had asked if my start date could be delayed until November, in order to sit exams for the Open University to complete my BSc course. Falklands Conservation had replied that it was imperative that I start in October, but told me that I could sit my exams at the Mount Pleasant Education Centre, situated in the military base 60 kilometres from Stanley. They even offered transportation for me to reach the centre.

The first few days after my arrival were mostly spent studying for my exams. The work paid off, because I passed both my exams at Distinction level, and was then free to concentrate on the task in hand.

My predecessor had left several months before my arrival, and my two assistants, Tim Stenning and Jeremy Smith, were both as new to the job as I was, so I was on a steep learning curve. Still, much of the work was along similar lines to my previous work in Hawaii, albeit with different species. The research was based around a seabird monitoring programme that covered one species of albatross and two species of penguin.

Each season a small number of breeding colonies were visited at the completion of egg-laying, and the number of occupied nests counted to determine the population size. Later in the season these same colonies were re-visited to count the number of fully grown chicks. The number of chicks was divided by the number of nests to determine how successful a season it had been in terms of reproduction. The work was exciting, and so began my love affair with penguins.

As a child I had always been fascinated by penguins. It was hard to think of these comical creatures as wild animals, capable of taking on the rigours of a dangerous and hostile environment. The Falklands was incredibly rich in wildlife, and held an abundance of penguins. At some sites the sheer numbers of penguins was truly breath-taking.

As I became more familiar with the work, I began to be concerned about the way that some of the monitoring was being conducted. Magellanic penguins were the only Falkland penguins that lived in burrows, and only a small proportion of their burrows were occupied each year, making nest counting difficult. Falklands Conservation had tackled this problem by mapping out a small section in the centre of the breeding colony, and putting a flipper band on every adult within that section. To my mind there were two fundamental problems with this approach.

Firstly, because the tiny study area covered only the densest part in the centre of the colony, it was not reflecting true changes in population size. Changes in population size would be reflected by changes in the overall size of the colony, not just density. Because the edges of the colonies were not being recorded, any changes in colony size could not be determined. It was rather like determining the population of a city by counting the houses in a single street.

Secondly, the only way that the bands could be read each year was by capturing the bird. This was achieved using a long wooden pole with a hook on the end, rather like a shepherd's crook. Each year the birds were hooked by the leg, and dragged out of their burrows just after egg-laying, so that the bands could be read.

This was so upsetting to the birds that the following day piles of soil would be seen outside the burrows, as panic stricken birds tried digging themselves in deeper. In many cases the birds were so upset that they kicked their eggs out of the burrow along with the soil. Clearly it was impossible to record breeding success, when the monitoring process was altering the results by destroying eggs.

One of the first things that I did was to halt the banding and capture of these penguins, and to change the form of monitoring. I set up new study plots that covered entire colonies, and used simple visual inspection to determine which burrows were occupied. Because the new study plots were now covering the entire colony, changes in population size could be recorded as the colony expanded or contracted. The new monitoring method also meant that the birds no longer needed to be handled.

Another concern was that out of the four species of penguin that lived in the Falkland Islands, only two were actually being monitored. Rockhopper penguins in particular had undergone a huge decline since the establishment of commercial fishing, with adults dying off in their thousands, and yet this species was curiously excluded from the Seabird Monitoring Programme. To my mind this represented a serious oversight, and I extended the programme to include all four species of penguin.

My final concern was something that was more difficult to resolve quickly. The whole Seabird Monitoring Programme was based on the assumption that the handful of colonies being monitored each year were reflective of changes within the entire Falklands population. For species that remained at fixed breeding sites this was perhaps a reasonable assumption, but for Gentoo penguins it was not.

Gentoo penguins move their colonies a short distance each year, and every so often entire colonies will disappear completely from a given location, with birds dispersing to alternative sites. Falklands Conservation had selected three sites at which to monitor Gentoo penguins; sites chosen because of their high concentrations of penguins. Because these sites already had very high concentrations of penguins, it was inevitable that decline would be observed as a result of random movement.

The only solution was to extend the number of sites being monitored to including smaller sites, and to combine this with a complete census of all the Falkland breeding sites. An island-wide census was the only way to determine whether changes in specially selected colonies were representative of the population as a whole. Clearly such a project would be a major undertaking, but I felt sure in my own mind that it could be done with sufficient planning.

With this in mind I instructed Tim Stenning and Jeremy Smith to conduct a census of all the Gentoo penguin colonies in East Falkland. This represented only a fraction of what would be required to undertake an island-wide census, but it would nevertheless give an indication as to the logistics of undertaking such a project. As it turned out the East Falkland census was completed in just two weeks. This convinced me that an island-wide penguin census was logistically feasible, but the project would have to wait until the funding became available.

The Falklands Conservation office at that time was just a portakabin, and our total annual budget was £32,000 ($45,000). The only computer in our possession was gathering dust in the corner because nobody knew how to use it. All the data that Falklands Conservation had gathered over the years was held on scraps of paper in filing cabinets. There were not even any data recording forms.

I made up some proper forms for recording data, and began looking at ways of entering the data onto a computer database. Unfortunately the office computer had no software for creating databases, so I purchased a computer of my own and the necessary software to do the job. I spent most of my spare time taking pieces of data from literally hundreds of pieces of loose paper, and gradually building up a database. Now at last population trends became apparent from the jumble of figures, and it became obvious that Rockhoppers were not the only penguins to have declined since the establishment of commercial fishing.

During early 1994, I discussed with Falklands Conservation the need to develop baseline survey techniques within the islands. Falklands Conservation's research programmes had previously concentrated on just penguins and albatross, but there was clearly a need to expand this research to cover other wildlife.

It was important to ensure that any baseline surveys were conducted according to internationally approved techniques, but in order to do this the habitat categories used in Britain needed to be altered to match the Falklands environment. Many habitat types found in the Falklands, such as Tussac grass, were not found in Britain and therefore needed to be added.

During January 1994 I conducted pilot surveys at various points around the islands, in order to establish what new categories were required. As a result of these studies, I put together a Baseline Survey Programme based on standardised methodology, but tailored to suit Falkland Islands habitats and species. The first baseline surveys were scheduled for the summer of 1994/95.

Baseline surveys could be conducted on very low budgets, since the only requirement was somebody qualified and experienced in doing such work, and a means of transport to reach the sites. I was therefore fairly confident of being able to get these surveys underway the following season.

The island-wide penguin census was a totally different proposition. In order to census so many sites in the space of a few weeks meant having several teams in operation. The large number of outer islands also meant that a boat would need to be chartered, and that would be expensive. Although Falklands Conservation were in the process of raising money through a Penguin Appeal, it was unlikely that this funding would be available until 1995 at the earliest. I therefore kept the idea on hold.

In early June I received a phone call from the hospital to say that I had failed the medical for my life insurance policy because I was anaemic. I was called in for a repeat blood test, and this showed an even lower blood count. After an examination by the doctor, I was referred to a surgeon, who discovered that I had a tumour in my intestinal area. Two days later, on 15th June 1994, I was admitted into hospital for surgery to remove the tumour.

By now I was a veteran of surgical operations, but nothing could have prepared me for how ill I was to feel. I awoke lying on my side, with a plastic tube going up my nose and down my throat. I felt terribly nauseous, and was continually vomiting, which was not helped by the tube down my throat. I also felt anxious, and felt my heart beating very erratically, producing an incredibly uncomfortable feeling in my chest that I just couldn't ease. I felt so uncomfortable and ill that I was unable to sleep for more than a few minutes at a time, despite being exhausted. Time passed dreadfully slowly.

The following Tuesday the surgeon came to visit me, and explained what had been done. Apparently a tumour the size of a large grapefruit had been found in my intestine, and this had attached itself to some of the adjacent organs. The surgeon had removed the tumour with about a metre of diseased intestine, and had removed all the remnants of the tumour that had been attached to other organs. He told me that he thought it very unlikely that the tumour was cancerous, but that he would send it away for examination just to be certain.

On the Wednesday, I discharged myself from hospital for a couple of hours in order to attend an important Tourist Board Meeting at the Falkland Islands Development Corporation offices. I was in some considerable discomfort, but managed to stay long enough to discuss the Guidelines for Wildlife Tourism which was the main issue relevant to my work.

The following Wednesday I was due to receive the results of the tests on the tumour, and I was very nervous. I had had a terrible dream the previous night that I had been diagnosed with cancer, and had to leave the Falklands. I thought that I was prepared for most eventualities, but I never expected the news that I received.

The section of intestine had been examined, and had revealed two separate tumours comprising two different types of cancer. I was diagnosed with a very aggressive Non-Hodgkins Lymphoma, which had formed the bulk of the tumour, and a much smaller and slower growing carcenoid. To be diagnosed with cancer was devastating enough, but to have two different types of cancer growing within a single tumour seemed hopeless.

I was told that immediate arrangements were being made for me to fly back to Britain to attend a specialist cancer ward at the Woolwich Hospital in London. I would then undergo a series of tests in order to determine my prognosis. I was stunned by the news, and went home to have a large whisky.

Having witnessed my mother being eaten away by cancer some 10 years before, I knew a fair bit about the disease and its treatments. Each type of cancer had its own form of treatment, and its own prognosis for survival. To expect to overcome two completely different forms seemed almost hopeless. I began to think more in terms of what I could achieve during my remaining time, rather than whether I could be cured. I spent the final few days publishing an article on my Rockhopper penguin findings, and on finishing off Falklands Conservation's display for Farmer's Week.

On Wednesday 6th July I finally left the Falklands, destined for who knows what. I had no idea whether I would ever see the Falklands and all my new friends again. Gone was the happiness that I had discovered in those wonderful islands. I kept asking myself why this should have happened to me, but there were no answers.

I finally arrived in Woolwich hospital, and soon began a series of tests. X-rays, blood tests, a CT scan and worst of all a bone marrow test. This involved taking a core sample of the bone marrow from my hip by cutting through the hip bone with a tiny boring tool. I was given a local anaesthetic, but this only numbs the skin, not the hip bone. Needless to say it was very painful, but very necessary.

On 20th July I finally got to see the doctor to hear the results of all my tests. The carcenoid had been removed completely, and was a very slow growing cancer, which the doctor reckoned could now be ignored. The other cancer was a lymphoma, and the tests had shown up no obvious signs of it having spread to other parts of the body. It was however a very aggressive form of cancer, and only required a few active cells to produce secondary tumours. In addition, the CT scan had shown some thickening around the area of surgery, which was possible evidence of further tumour cells.

In view of the very real risk that the lymphoma was still present in my body, the doctor recommended a course of chemotherapy. I knew a little about this from my mother's illness, but was very surprised to discover that I was to undergo chemotherapy for 4 months. I was to receive a concentrated dose of chemotherapy every Tuesday for 16 weeks.

Because my lymphoma was such an aggressive strain, it was important to try and hit it as hard as possible with the strongest form of chemotherapy that I could withstand. If after a couple of weeks the chemotherapy proved to be too much for me cope with, then the potency would be reduced, but of course so too would the prospects of success and ultimate survival. The only good news was that aggressive forms of cancer, such as my lymphoma, responded better to chemotherapy than non-aggressive forms of cancer.

And so on Tuesday 26th July I began my first dose of chemotherapy. A catheter was put into the vein on my arm, and this was connected up to a large bag of saline solution containing the chemotherapy. For the first hour or so I felt fine, and I began to hope that I would not react badly to it, but then I started to feel really unwell.

I began to feel very nauseous, but it was much worse than normal nausea that one might expect if one has a hang-over from drinking too much. I began to feel, smell and taste the putrid chemicals coursing through my body. It was as though I had some strange chemical compound in my mouth that I could not spit out, but of course it wasn't in my mouth, it was in my blood stream.

My heart began to beat erratically, and I began to sweat profusely even though I was cold. Even my sweat stank of the horrid chemicals, and I began to vomit uncontrollably. For hours I continued to vomit, as my body tried to evict poisons which it assumed had originated from something I ate. The doctor explained that the chemotherapy was indeed a poison, and that the treatment aimed to strike a balance between killing the cancer cells and not killing the patient.

I continued to vomit throughout the following day, even though there was nothing left in my stomach to come up. Eventually the constant wrenching ruptured delicate blood vessels in my throat, causing me to vomit blood as well as bile.

I remained in this awful state for two days, and then began to recover. I eventually felt well enough to leave the hospital for a few days, and spent the weekend with my aunt Anne in the New Forest. I felt so relieved to be over the sickness. I tried to convince myself that the first dose would be the worst, and that the subsequent treatments would be less traumatic. Unfortunately that wasn't the case.

I returned to hospital the following Tuesday, and was given my second dose of chemotherapy. Once again I was dreadfully ill for two days, and by now I was starting to feel really low. I just couldn't see how I could go through another 14 weeks of it. The hospital was so far away from family that they were unable to visit much, and I really needed somebody to keep my spirits up.

By the end of the fourth dose the side-effects were really starting to take hold. In addition to the weekly vomiting which followed each treatment, I was beginning to feel very weak, my hair was beginning to fall out, and I began to lose the feeling in my fingers. Areas of sensitive skin were also starting to break down. The skin around my mouth began cracking and splitting, and I developed numerous ulcers. Even worse was that the skin around my anus did the same. Every time I moved my bowels, the skin would split open and bleed profusely, causing intolerable agony for hours afterwards. The pain was so bad that I was unable to sit, stand, lie or sleep. All I wanted to do was curl up in a corner and die.

I wanted to tell the doctor to ease off the treatment, or even to stop it altogether and let me take my chances. Life is precious, but at what cost? As it was I felt so ill each time I had the chemotherapy, that I would have gladly died to have stopped the suffering.

On the fourth weekend I went to see my sister Alison and her husband Martin in Canterbury. I had to go everywhere by train, and this time the journey caused me to relapse. I was sick on the platform, and had to be helped back onto the train. I barely slept for vomiting that night, and by now my throat was bleeding again. A local doctor was called out, and I was given an injection to try and control the vomiting.

By now I was a quarter of the way through my treatment, and feeling at my lowest. I still had a very long way to go in my treatment, and yet by now my strength to fight the drugs had become completely drained. The pain from the splitting skin around my anus and mouth was excruciating, and none of the pain killers I was given made any difference at all. To top it all, my next CT scan was still four weeks away, a long time to wait to discover whether the treatment was working - whether I was going to live or die.

I was in such agony from the breakdown of my skin, that each day was a nightmare. This was punctuated by the need to drag myself back to hospital to have more poisons pumped into my veins, knowing that they would make me sicker than somebody who has never undergone chemotherapy could ever imagine. On top of it all was the knowledge that it was probably all for nothing; that sooner or later I would fall victim to the same horrible death as my mother had.

I had run out of physical strength, and the will to fight on. I was still convinced that my chances of fighting off two forms of cancer were slim, and that the hell I was going through was probably all for nothing. I began making plans for the day when the doctors finally told me it was hopeless. I told the doctors that I had difficulty in sleeping because of the worry, and they prescribed two sleeping tablets a day. I did not actually take any of these tablets, but stored them up for the day when I would need them to end my suffering.

When I returned to the hospital the following Tuesday I felt very low. My blood tests showed that I had become very anaemic as a result of constant bleeding from the splits in my anus and mouth. I was given my chemotherapy, and then a blood transfusion that lasted 11 hours. By Thursday I felt up to leaving the hospital, and returned to Martin and Alison's house.

They were wonderful in letting me go there whenever I wanted. It was so important for me to get away from the hospital as soon as I could each week. The ward was a special cancer ward, and being surrounded by the smell of chemotherapy, and other patients dying from cancer did nothing to help my nausea or my moral.

The blood transfusion had boosted my red blood cell count, but in order to overcome the damage being done by the chemotherapy to my white blood cells, I was given hormone injections to stimulate white cell production. I had to administer these injections to myself, and the injections were put into the stomach. It was not very pleasant, but I managed.

With nothing else to do but dwell on my suffering, I worked on my computer, drafting the coming season's fieldwork schedule for Falklands Conservation. It was looking increasingly doubtful that I would be back in time to start the fieldwork, and I was the only employee with experience enough to plan the work schedule. I did not want the research to suffer as a result of my illness, so I wrote out a very detailed step by step schedule for other members of staff to follow, and faxed it to the office.

I also transferred all the hand-written fieldwork notes, from the past 5 years of seabird research, onto the computer databases that I had designed. At each stage of the process I discovered patterns and trends which had been completely overlooked whilst the data had remained on scraps of paper. I wrote a number of articles on the discoveries I had made, and sent them to Stanley for publication.

I eventually reached the mid-way point in my chemotherapy, and was sent for another CT scan. This scan showed the thickening around the area of surgery to be very much as it had been before. Nobody seemed to know for certain what this meant, but the hope was that it was just scar tissue rather than remaining cancer cells. In view of this, the chemotherapy was to continue as planned for another eight weeks.

I was optimistic that the treatment was working, but concerned by how vague the diagnosis of the thickened intestinal wall had been. Nevertheless, I still had eight more weeks of treatment to go. I kept telling myself that if I had already done eight weeks, that I could do another eight. In reality this was not the case. Even if my moral held out, I was not sure that my body would. Each week I became weaker and in still greater pain.

The bleeding from the cracks in my anus had got progressively worse, and I was now needing blood transfusions every second week. The pain was still unbearable, and even the strongest painkillers that the doctor could offer made little difference. Every time I moved my bowels the skin would split open again, causing uncontrolled bleeding and incredible pain.

By now all my hair had fallen out, and my nails were also changing colour. The skin in my mouth and throat had broken down, making eating and swallowing painful, and I permanently felt as though I was suffering from sea sickness. I was also starting to feel completely worn out. I had no energy, my breathing was laboured, my heart beat was erratic and my vision had begun to go blurry. In addition my nerves were becoming damaged to the extent that I was unable to use my fingers properly. It became a real struggle just to do up a button.

All of these were on a good day - a day that I was not continually vomiting from the effects of a dose of chemotherapy. I could not see how my body would hold out for a further 8 weeks. With every week that passed I became sicker and weaker.

I had now reached a point whereby my digestive system shut down on Tuesdays. I would try to eat a good breakfast on Tuesday morning, knowing that it would be my last meal for a couple of days. By the time I reached the hospital in the late afternoon I would begin to feel sick. So fearful of the treatment had I become, that I would start vomiting before the chemotherapy had even begun, and the food that I had eaten hours before was completely undigested. Apparently this was perfectly normal a few weeks into the treatment.

The nurse told me that so horrific was this form of chemotherapy, that patients often suffered bouts of vomiting months or even years afterwards whenever they recalled their treatment. She told me how she had once met an ex-patient in the shopping centre two years after his treatment. As soon as the patient recognised her and remembered the chemotherapy, he had thrown up in the street.

Other people embarking on chemotherapy who might read this should not despair though, because each type of chemotherapy is unique. Mine was the most potent and toxic form, aimed at killing a very aggressive form of cancer. Other types of chemotherapy have much less severe side-effects.

As a welcome break to the routine, I had an invitation to the opening of an art exhibition in aid of Falklands Conservation's Penguin Appeal, in the Ecology Centre in London. It was to be attended by Prince Andrew and Sir David Attenborough, and I particularly wanted to meet Sir David Attenborough. Fortunately it was on a Monday, which gave me the longest possible time to recover from my weekly treatment.

I was staying with Alison and Martin in Canterbury that weekend, and Alison came along as my guest. I met Prince Andrew very briefly, but had a good long chat to Sir David Attenborough about wildlife in the Falklands. He was very interested in the Falklands, having just completed work on the wildlife documentary series "Life in the Freezer". It was a very interesting discussion, with a man who was every bit as charismatic in person as he was on television.

By now it was October, and I could see the light at the end of the tunnel, if only I could hold out physically. I was now receiving blood transfusions every few days, and having to inject myself in the stomach with increasing quantities of hormones to stimulate white blood cell production. With such a low white blood cell count, the doctors feared that I would pick up an infection that my body would be unable to fight, but so far I had managed to avoid any serious infections.

My fingernails had become increasingly discoloured throughout my chemotherapy. In early November, I was closing the door of my aunt's car when I ripped the nail back along its entire length, causing it to bleed profusely. The nail was left hanging by a small piece of skin, but I managed to fold it back down and bind it up with my handkerchief until I could get to the doctor. The doctor simply put a plaster over it to hold it in place.

When I looked at my other nails, I could see that the reason they had changed colour was because they had become detached from the underlying skin. All my nails were in fact only held in place at the point of growth, and any one of them could have been ripped back by the slightest pressure. In order to stop any of the other nails being torn off, I trimmed them back to about half their normal length, so that they were cut well short of the end of my finger. It looked silly having the ends of my fingers with no nails, but it was better than having them torn out.

On Tuesday 8th November, I had my last treatment of chemotherapy. As usual I was violently sick for two days, but finally I left the hospital for the last time, and returned to Canterbury. On Monday 14th November, Alison and Martin drove me to Brize Norton, where I caught the plane back to the Falklands. I gave them both a huge hug, and thanked them for all their support. Without my weekend escapes from the hospital, my moral would have withered away completely. I owed a huge debt of gratitude to all my family.

As I boarded the plane destined for the Falkland Islands, I closed the book on the worst nightmare I could have imagined. If I had ever known that my chemotherapy could have been so bad and so painful, I can honestly say that I would never have begun it in the first place. If I lived to enjoy fifty deliriously happy years as a result of the treatment, it would still not make the pain and suffering worthwhile.

The treatment all but broke me. It damaged me both physically and emotionally, and confirmed my belief that there are times when death really is preferable to life. In the back of my mind I could not dismiss the knowledge that I had only delayed the inevitable. Just like my mother before me, one day I would have to face my cancer again.

CHAPTER ELEVEN

Although it was wonderful to get back to the Falklands, I did not find myself jumping for joy as I might have expected. I was actually in quite a depressed state, and finding it difficult to pick up the pieces.

I still suffered from many of the side-effects, but was assured that these would gradually ease off now that the chemotherapy had stopped. The main problem however, was that I was unable to think in terms of having a future. I was quite convinced that sooner or later the cancer would return, and I found it difficult to make long term plans.

The fieldwork programme that I had drawn up was already underway by the time I arrived in the Falklands. Fortunately Tim Stenning had worked with us the year before, and was therefore familiar with the work. He was more than capable of undertaking the fieldwork without supervision, and had Steve Bronie as an assistant. Jeremy Smith, our assistant from the previous season, was no longer working with Falklands Conservation, and was in Britain doing an MSc course. Apart from myself, Tim was the only experienced research worker, and his presence was invaluable following my illness.

I still had an obligation to get the Baseline Survey Programme underway, and the bulk of this work needed to be done during January and early February. Tim seemed able to maintain the Seabird Monitoring Programme with Steve Bronie, which left me free to plan and conduct the Baseline Survey work.

I began with some trial surveys around Hearndon Water and Penarrow Point, in order to ensure that everything worked according to plan. Then in January 1995 I began my Baseline Survey of Berkeley Sound.

This was no small task. The aim was to walk over 100 kilometres of coastline twice, first along the beach itself, and then back through the vegetation that lay behind the beach. All the vegetation types and coastline geology were to be mapped out, and every single bird and mammal encountered during the survey was to be recorded in its exact location on the map.

Penguin populations can be easily counted because they breed together in densely packed colonies, but most other coastal species are widely scattered along the coastline, making colony counts impossible. These species can only be counted by recording the total number of breeding pairs along very long lengths of coastline. Having established breeding density, in terms of nests per kilometre of coastline, it is then possible to repeat the count in future years to determine any population change. These data can also be overlaid onto maps of vegetation and coastline types, to show which habitats are favoured by each species.

I set off alone on Tuesday 10th January 1995, my elderly Landrover loaded up with camping gear in the back and my motorcycle mounted on the front. I was immediately faced by the challenge of crossing Drunken Rock Pass. This was the only point at which the Murrell River could be crossed by vehicle, but the ground was very soft, and I got stuck in the mud before I even reached the river. After 40 minutes spent digging and putting boards under the wheels, I finally reached the river.

Old vehicle tracks cut into the bank showed me where to enter the river, but there was nothing obvious on the other side. A young lad called Joe Clarke had come down from one of the farms on his motorcycle, and was waiting to greet me on the other side of the bank, so I headed towards where he was waiting. The river was high, and water soon covered the floor of the vehicle, but I had to keep going. I reached the other bank, and immediately got bogged again. I could now see that the ground where I was bogged was not in fact the opposite bank, but a small islet running adjacent to the bank. I still had another 100 metres or so to reach the other side of the river.

Joe waited patiently as I dug out the Landrover yet again, but eventually I did reach him on the far side. I followed him to Murrell Farm where I was greeted with a very welcome cup of coffee. This would be the last settlement that I would encounter during my journey along the north coast of Port William. I reached the bottom of Mount Low shortly before dusk, and set up camp.

Being on my own, I didn't bother to pitch a tent, I simply laid out my sleeping bag in the back of the Landrover. I could see the lights of Stanley twinkling in the distance across the Sound, and I savoured the peace and tranquillity. The stars shone brightly above me, and the night air was alive with the call of night flying snipe.

Working alone did not really bother me, in fact I preferred it. Baseline surveying was a skilled job, and required utmost concentration. One needed to be very silent and alert when seeking out breeding birds, and going around in pairs was not conducive to stealth and quiet. I was also a fairly solitary person in many ways. Ever since my disfigurement as a teenager, I had found it difficult to feel at ease with strangers. This was partly because I felt uncomfortable about my appearance, and partly because of shyness. I think many people mistook this for unfriendliness, but it wasn't.

I had always been shy even as a teenager, but the death of Jackie, and my subsequent disfigurement had taken this shyness to an extreme. I was a very confident person in most respects, but not with personal relationships. Other people tend to sense when somebody feels uneasy, and pull away from such situations. Such reactions only serve to reinforce ones feelings of inadequacy.

My cancer had also changed my outlook towards life, but not for the better. I had become only too aware of my mortality, and felt as though my remaining life was going to be short. My unfulfilled dreams became so much more urgent, as I was only too aware that time was running out.

Of these unfulfilled dreams, the loss of Jackie and our baby weighed heaviest on my mind. Whilst I was happy to dedicate my life to wildlife conservation, I felt a burning need to find love and companionship with a sole-mate such as I had lost.

My other burning desire was to do something useful with my life. My interest in wildlife conservation had always been very strong, and my desire to achieve something significant in this field was another driving force. It was for this reason that I had spent much of my own money purchasing a computer, motorcycle and field equipment essential to getting Falklands Conservation's new projects up and running.

Falklands Conservation were receiving an annual budget of just £30,000 (US$45,000), and this was not enough to pay for things that were needed for the projects. I constantly thought about the island-wide penguin census that I wanted to conduct. It seemed as though the only way that I was likely to get such a project going for the 1995/96 season would be to fund it myself. I had estimated that the entire project could be carried out for around £20,000 (US$30,000), and I knew that I could afford this. I had in fact just received an inheritance of over £20,000 from my grandmother, and I decided that I would use this to fund the project.

There was no denying that such a project would be a milestone in penguin conservation. The Falklands was such an important location for penguins, and yet nobody could even say how many penguins there were. Without any population data it was impossible to determine the level of threat from commercial fishing and oil exploration. An island-wide census would provide a baseline figure against which future changes could be compared. It would be a piece of work that would take its place in history.

But for now the business of getting the Baseline Survey Project up and running was the priority. This work was no less important. It was the first step in providing baseline data on species other than penguins. This data would also provide a baseline against which future change could be measured, albeit on a more lowly scale than my proposed penguin census.

The following day I broke camp and drove on to Kidney Cove; the southern entrance to Berkeley Sound, and the starting point for my survey. After setting up camp, I walked down the coastline mapping out which areas of coastline had cliffs, sand, stones, boulders or estuarine mud, and which areas held important biological associations such as mussels or seaweeds. I also recorded the location of every single bird or mammal observed, and whether they were breeding or just present. On the return journey, I walked a couple of hundred metres behind the coastline, mapping out the vegetation types, and recording wildlife present.

I was generally able to survey around 4 kilometres of coastline per day, although this was very dependant upon the type of coastline. Sections of cliff were much slower, due to the need to traverse up and down every gully in search of hidden Rock Shags, Steamer Ducks and Kelp Geese. I took climbing ropes and wedges so that I could gain access to particularly difficult sections of cliff, although the cliffs along Berkeley Sound were not generally too difficult to negotiate.

At times I became aware that I was conducting my fieldwork in a manner that could only be described as reckless, especially bearing in mind that I was totally alone in an area that was very remote. Climbing down cliff faces to search for seabirds could easily have resulted in a slip that would have left me stranded and possibly injured. I had anticipated being away for a couple of weeks at a time, so help would not have been forthcoming for a considerable time.

To suggest that my dedication to the work outweighed my personal safety would be misleading. I have never considered myself to be heroic, and there were many occasions when I was very scared, and had to really force myself to continue. But I always had at the back of my mind that to die for something I believed in, was preferable to dying from cancer. I was much more afraid of dying from cancer than of dying from a fall.

When I had finished surveying as far as the bottom of Mount Low, I had to return along my previous route, and cross over the Saddle towards Long Island. I had been told that there was an old abandoned track that could be followed, but it had been disused for so long that it soon became impossible to trace. I knew generally which direction I needed to follow, but without knowing the correct route it was inevitable that I would reach marshes and river valleys that were impassable by Landrover.

I followed the line of telegraph poles which I knew headed towards Long Island farm, but found my route blocked on several occasions by rivers and marshland. After back-tracking several times to get around these natural obstructions, I eventually arrived at Strike Off Point and set up camp.

During the night there was torrential rain, and when it finally stopped on Sunday afternoon, the ground was sodden. I did my survey of the surrounding area, and then moved on to Long Island farm. I was now back on a recognisable track, but it was on a steep grassy slope, and the heavy rain had made it treacherous.

I reached one particularly difficult section, where I had to drive down a steep muddy slope, which now had a stream running across it from the rain. The Landrover started to become unstable because of the incline, and began sliding off the greasy track towards the edge. I managed to stop the slide, but by now the vehicle had left the track, and was lying at a very precarious angle. I tried to creep along the grass slowly in order to get back up onto the track, but the vehicle lifted onto two wheels as it verged on the point of toppling down hill. I got it back onto all four wheels by steering down hill again, but that left me still further from the track, and closer to the edge. I was now on very slippery grass, which inclined steeply away towards the cliff edge. Each time I turned back towards the track, the Landrover began to lean dangerously once more, and threatened to topple over.

I got out and had a look to see just how near it was to toppling over. I tried to estimate where the centre of gravity lay, in order to determine whether unloading the vehicle would help or not. I decided that it probably would, although it was doubtful that it would help much.

I emptied out all the gear, and then tried once more to t ck across the slope, in order to reach the track. Occ sionally the lower wheels would go down a holl w, causing the higher wheels to lift as it balanced on two wheels. Each time I had to correct it by steering down hill, and each time this put me nearer to the edge, and pointing down hill once more.

It was completely impossible to reverse back up the hill, since the wet grass gave me no grip. The best I could do was to drive parallel to the edge, holding my contour, and trying to avoid depressions that could have tipped the Landrover past its centre of gravity. If it had not been for the fact that the track was going down hill, I doubt I would have reached it. As it was I managed to edge my way along until the track finally joined the cliff top, and I managed to get back on to it. I was very relieved, having had visions of losing the Landrover over the edge, possible with myself inside it.

From there on the track improved, and eventually I reached the settlement at Long Island, and was welcomed by Neil and Glenda Watson. I spent another three days surveying around Long Island, and headed home to Stanley along the gravel road, having completed half the survey.

The second half of the survey along the north coast of Berkeley Sound passed without incident until almost the very end. As I was working my way homewards I reached Fish Creek, the head of an estuary which is regularly crossed by Landrover at low tide. I tried following the tracks of a previous vehicle, but suddenly nose-dived into a muddy hollow. I got out of the Landrover to take a look.

The front axle had disappeared from sight into the mud, whilst the rear wheels were still high and dry on bedrock. There was insufficient traction on the slippery rock to pull the front end out of the mud, so I set to work with spade and boards. There was now only a couple of hours of daylight remaining, and the tide was starting to come back in. Time was running out. Within a couple of hours the area where the Landrover was stranded would be flooded, and I was making no progress at all freeing the front wheels. I stood back to assess the situation.

The hollow was so soft and wet that it gave little purchase to the jack or boards. On the other hand, the fact that the rear wheels were on firm ground meant that I could reverse out of the hollow if I had more traction. What I needed was another vehicle to tow me out, and I decided that my best chance of success lay in running across to Port Louis settlement, which was about 4 kilometres away.

I was delighted to find Mike and Sue Morrison at home. Without hesitation Mike drove me back out to Fish Creek, and we connected up his vehicle to mine with a tow rope. With both vehicles in 4 wheel-drive, my Landrover popped straight out, accompanied by a horrendous odour from the black anaerobic mud which now coated the front.

I thanked Mike enthusiastically, and apologised for my stupidity at getting into such a situation. He went back home to get his long overdue supper, and I pressed on to find a suitable camp site before dark. I finally completed my epic survey on the 2nd of February, and spent a few days resting at home.

By 7th February I went out to Westpoint Island to begin a similar survey. Berkeley Sound had been an ideal coastline survey, but Westpoint offered an even greater challenge, since I wanted to experiment with conducting transect counts of inland birds, in order to estimate their populations on small islands. Westpoint was an ideal size to try out such a survey.

I was met at the tiny airstrip by Roddy and Lily Napier. As usual I was given a very warm welcome, and on this occasion they had even prepared me a room in their own house, so as to save me living alone in the guest house.

Westpoint was perhaps my favourite spot in all of the Falklands. Not only were Roddy and Lily so friendly, but the island had a sense of peace and tranquillity about it that I had experienced at few other places. After a long day's work, I would often return to the Devil's Nose and spend an hour or two amongst the penguins and albatross reflecting on my life and the personal difficulties that I faced.

My survey went very much to plan, and a week later I returned to Stanley. My efforts were now concentrated on more mundane matters, such as replacing our portakabin with a proper office, and employing a new member of staff to promote environmental education.

On March 19th I heard that Roddy had been rushed into hospital with a ruptured appendix. It was ironic that only a few weeks before he had told me that the only way he would ever leave Westpoint Island again would be feet first. When I first saw him he looked very ill, but as the days went by he looked more and more like his old self, and we spent many an hour talking about wildlife and the Falklands. There were few people whose opinion I respected more, and few people whose friendship I valued greater. I visited him virtually every day whilst he was in hospital, and whilst he was at his Stanley home recuperating.

On 29th March I went out to Westpoint to do the final seabird counts of the season. I also promised Roddy that I would help with a few of the jobs which needed doing about the farm while he was laid up in hospital. These jobs included servicing the Landrovers, and shearing a few of the sheep that had been missed. Alan White had also gone out to Westpoint to keep things ticking over in Roddy's absence, and between us we set about trying to round up the stray sheep.

We had three of Roddy's dogs to help. Two of these were inexperienced, and spent most of the time running about scattering the sheep, in complete disregard of our instructions. The old dog Rope was excellent, but he could only run for a short while before becoming tired, so we ended up running him about in the Landrover, and putting him out to run each time we really needed him. We finally got the stray sheep into the pen ready for shearing.

Before we could begin shearing we had to sharpen up the shearing blades, and the only grinder available to do this was an old petrol machine that pre-dated the Ark. The grinding wheel was driven by a petrol motor, and the petrol tank sat over the top of the motor, leaking petrol all over the place as it ran. Sparks off the grinding wheel flew up all over the leaky petrol tank, and how the whole thing never burst into flames I will never know.

I returned to Stanley on 2nd April, and shortly afterwards Roddy was taken into hospital again for another operation. On 13th April I put my proposal for an island-wide penguin census to the Falklands Conservation committee, and they were very keen on the idea. In fact the only doubts expressed were by those who thought such a feat would be impossible. I assured them that with careful planning it could be done, and gave them a brief outline of the cost. It was suggested that money recently donated by the Wellcome Foundation could be used for the project, in which case I would not have to use my own money.

Shortly after this meeting I had to return to Britain to have my first check-up since finishing my chemotherapy. These tests showed no signs of any cancer, and I breathed a huge sigh of relief.

Whilst I was in Britain I attended a meeting with the UK trustees of Falklands Conservation to present my penguin census proposal. They were also enthusiastic about the project, and I began to work on some of the logistical details. This included purchasing another off-road motorcycle to be sent to the Falklands, since each of the two land-based census teams would need one to reach the more remote colonies.

After two weeks in Britain I flew to New York to attend a conference being held by the Wildlife Conservation Society. I was to give a lecture on seabird research in the Falkland Islands. I stayed at the hotel St. Moritz on the Park, so named because it was directly across the street from Central Park.

Due to the time shift from Britain I found myself waking up at 4am each morning, and this allowed me to see Central Park at its finest. Each morning I went around the corner for breakfast at 4am, and then went for a stroll around the park. It was so peaceful and tranquil at that time of the morning. The trees and lakes were shrouded in mist, and the birds and squirrels were going about their business oblivious to my presence.

I wandered around the deserted skating rink, and the Carousel, dedicated to a dead child called Michelle, who according to the plaque "had loved the pretty horses". I could relate to the heartbreak of the bereaved parents who had placed the plaque there, and felt more than a little melancholy. There was not a sole about. At about 6am the joggers began emerging by the dozen, and by 7am it was mayhem. Time to return to the hotel for the "official" breakfast.

The room was paid for by the Wildlife Conservation Society, which was just as well since it cost several hundred dollars a night. Breakfast was similarly priced, and I limited myself to a pot of coffee. Even that was $10. When I happened to mention my 5am walks through Central Park, alone, the organisers were horrified, and alerted me to the dangers of street gangs and drug dealers who frequented the park.

The conference went very well, and I was pleased with my presentation. On the final day we were given a guided tour around Bronx Zoo, which was truly awesome. With the conference over I had one full day in New York before returning home, and I decided to go back to get a proper look around the Zoo. I used the tube-train to get there, which was quite an experience in itself. As I sat in a carriage full of people passing through the Bronx, it dawned on me that I was the only white person in the carriage. I have never been a racist, and the fact that I was the only white person was more of a surprise than a concern. I had been taught a very harrowing lesson about racism as a child, and I have never forgotten it.

I used to play cricket for my school, and one day as we were on our way to the cricket ground in Whalley Range, we came across an accident that had just happened. A black boy of around 8 or 9 years of age had just been hit by a car and was lying in the road. A couple of people were trying to help him, and we just looked on in horror. The poor boy's eyes were wide with terror as his life's blood ran from his open torso. He knew he was dying, and his expression told of the fear he was experiencing during his last moments of life.

As we turned away our teacher said to us, "Don't worry about it. It's just one less black bastard in the world."

Some of my friends laughed, but I felt such a feeling of disgust that a fellow human being could have been so unconcerned by what he had just witnessed.

CHAPTER TWELVE

On 26th May I returned to the Falklands, and set about getting the office computer up and running. It had never been loaded with Windows because the experts had said it did not have enough memory, but I managed to install the Windows software which I had purchased for my own machine, and soon had it running an office suite with database facility. Up until now I had had to do all the data analysis on my own computer, which meant I had had to do it all in my own time at home. Now I could finish it in work time.

The next few months were spent writing up the results of my baseline survey work, and making preparations for the forthcoming island-wide penguin census. The census required a huge amount of planning because it was such a mammoth project. Over a hundred breeding sites needed to be visited and counted in a four week period, and many of the sites were in remote locations or on outer islands.

I decided that the core of the work would be done by three teams. I would cover East Falkland by Landrover and motorcycle by myself, Jeremy and Sinead Smith would do the same for West Falkland, and Mike Riddy and an assistant would visit all the outer islands by boat. Two of the largest islands, Saunders Island and Pebble Island, were to be counted by the RAF Ornithological Society, who sent a separate team to each of the two islands. I also managed to recruit an RAF Hercules to fly me over the Jason Islands in order to obtain aerial photographs of these very large colonies.

In late October everything was set, and the teams started their counts simultaneously. I was covering the whole of East Falkland by myself, but I was also co-ordinating the whole effort through constant visits to the office in Stanley, so as to keep all the teams running smoothly. I began by counting the large Gentoo penguin colonies at Bull Point, and then back-tracked to count the colonies at Moffat Harbour. On the track out to Moffat Harbour I got badly bogged trying to cross a ditch, and lost several hours digging the Landrover out.

It is at times like this that you really miss a companion. Preferably one with a strong back.

With the Landrover free again, I could see no way of crossing the ditch with the Landrover, so I pressed on with the motorcycle, which I carried on the front of the Landrover for just such occasions. I reached the harbour and went to where the penguin colonies should have been, but there was no sign of them.

The colony location had been recorded only the year before, and even if the colony had moved there should have been a worn patch from the previous year's site, but I could find nothing. I rode around the harbour, constantly checking the map. I had the old farmhouse as a reference point, and all the features were just as they should have been, but no penguins.

Out of desperation I rode the bike up to the top of the nearby hill to get a bird's eye view. The harbour and farmhouse lay below me just as they should, but now I could see another house in the distance. After carefully studying the map the situation became clear. The house below me was not in fact Moffat Harbour House, but Danson Harbour House. The house in the distance was Moffat Harbour House. I was in the wrong section of coastline altogether. The shapes of the two harbours and the locations of the respective houses in each harbour were sufficiently similar that I had convinced myself that I had been in the right place. After another two hours over bumpy ground I finally reached the penguin colony, and managed to get back to the Landrover just before dark.

The remainder of the trip went without a hitch, and I had finished the census of the southern half of

East Falkland after just 9 days. I returned to Stanley to check on how the other teams were progressing, and was pleased to hear that they were all on schedule.

The Landrover I was using had been condemned by the local garage the previous season. We had been sent a replacement Landrover by our UK office, but due to various problems it had been despatched too late to arrive for the start of my census work. It had been rescheduled to arrive on 8th November, so I went to the port to collect it.

We had been assured by Ann Brown, the UK secretary, that it was in excellent condition with just 60,000 kilometres and a full service history. I had asked her to get it professionally inspected prior to shipment, and she had assured me that she would. I was therefore horrified to discover that the vehicle was a wreck.

The engine had been built up out of a cylinder head and engine block that did not match. This had left a pipe coming from the cylinder head which did not have anywhere to connect to at the other end. To overcome this problem the culprit had put the tube into a plastic drinks bottle which had been wired to the engine. This bottle melted during the four kilometre journey from the port to the Falklands Conservation office.

The wiring was faulty, the exhaust was broken and falling off, the steering linkages were bent, and the engine poured blue smoke out of the exhaust. The vehicle was a complete wreck, and I wrote to Ann Brown to tell her so. I suggested to the local trustees that the only thing to do with the vehicle was to return it for a full refund. In my opinion it was beyond economic repair, and we had clearly been swindled.

On closer inspection the engine and gearbox numbers did not agree with those we had bought, and we discovered that the original engine and gearbox had been stolen and replaced with a worn out assembly. Needless to say the professional inspection that I had requested, which Ann Brown had forgotten to undertake, would have picked up these faults. We later discovered that Ann Brown had bought the vehicle from a 'friend'. I began to suspect that some underhand dealing had taken place to substitute £6,000 of charity funds for a clapped out Landrover that was barely worth its weight in scrap. I appealed to the Falklands Conservation trustees involved, John Croxall, Ann Brown and Julian Fitter, to report the matter to police, but they refused. They even refused to return the vehicle to the supplier for a refund, for reasons known only to themselves.

As a result I was forced to resume my fieldwork in the old condemned Landrover. I set out to cover the North West section of East Falkland, and this took 10 days in all. I was back in Stanley again by 20th November.

By the end of November the boat survey of the islands had been completed, and the West Falklands team finished shortly afterwards. The only part of the project which remained was the aerial photography of the Jason Islands in order to assist mapping out these very large colonies. This was carried out a few days later in a Royal Air Force plane called a Hercules.

I was strapped into a harness with the side door open so that I could take a series of overlapping photographs as we flew along the cliff face where the penguins and albatross were nesting. The pilot clearly enjoyed the challenge of undertaking such a manoeuvre, and we approached each section of coast like a bombing run. I would never have believed that such a large plane could be so manoeuvrable. I was literally pinned to the floor by the force of gravity, unable to move, as we banked around to get into position for the first run along the northern cliff-face of Steeple Jason.

Diving down to about 70 metres above sea-level, we were so close to the cliff that I felt I could almost reach out and touch the birds. I clicked away with the camera on autowind taking a series of overlapping pictures along the length of the cliff-face. The pilot was flying as close to stall speed as possible to make it easier to get the pictures, but the turbulence was causing us to drop 30 metres at a time. At just 70 metres above the water that didn't give much room for error. The prospect of a bird striking an engine just didn't bear thinking about. These were brave guys.

"I hope you got that." the pilot sighed over the intercom, as we pulled up at the end of the run. "We can't do that again."

It was only later that they told me just how close we had been to ditching in the sea because of the severe turbulence. Fortunately the remaining cliffs were at a different orientation to the wind, and did not suffer from turbulence to the same degree. For these easier sections I was afforded the luxury of two runs per site, just to make sure that the photographs overlapped properly.

I can't thank the pilots of the Royal Air Force enough for the great job that they did, and the photographs that I obtained were superb. I could literally lay each set of photographs out and tape them together, to give one long picture of the length of the cliff-face. Some of the photographs were so clear that the individual nests could be counted, but all that was really needed was to be able to map out the areas that the colonies were occupying. The photographs more than served that purpose.

With the aerial work now done, all that remained was for me to co-ordinate the census results, add up the totals for all the colonies, and write a final report. This was one chapter of my life with which I felt immensely proud. Seabird researchers for years to come would be able to refer to this historic piece of work, and would be able to determine exactly whether penguin populations had gone up or down since this census had been taken. I had achieved the goal that I had set myself almost two years before, and had achieved it through the hard work and dedication of more than a hundred people. Employees, volunteers, military personnel, landowners and members of the general public had all participated. One participant wrote to us and told us that the projects' greatest achievement was the way in which it had brought together people from all walks of life to achieve a common goal.

The success of the project attracted a lot of media attention, and on 9th December 1995 I went out to Volunteer Point to conduct an interview about penguins for the BBC's Natural History Programme. The interview was recorded sitting close to one of the King penguin colonies, and we were continually interrupted by King penguin chicks climbing over our legs, probing our boot laces and hair with their bills, and tripping over our microphone lead.

My baseline survey work the previous year had also received government approval, and I was contracted by the Falkland Islands Government to conduct similar surveys at a number of locations around the Falklands as part of a major contract between the Falkland Islands Government, Falklands Conservation and Brown & Root.

The day after Christmas I decided to get started on one of these sites, the coastline around Mare Harbour and Bertha's beach. Mare Harbour was the military port, where all the war ships were moored: an area that was supposed to have high security. I couldn't have looked more suspicious, walking around the warships, fuel depots and military facilities, notebook and pen in one hand, and binoculars in the other. Every so often I would stop and survey the surroundings with my binoculars, and scribble down my findings on the map. I felt sure that somebody would eventually stop me to ask what I was doing, but they never did.

With the fieldwork and baseline surveys finally completed in February 1996, I wrote up the findings of our penguin census and presented them to government. The findings were alarming. Comparing population studies conducted by the British government in 1984 (Croxall, McInnes and Prince 1984 *"The status and conservation of seabirds at the Falkland Islands"*, ICBP Technical Publication No.2, British Antarctic Survey, Cambridge) with our 1996 census report, penguins in the Falklands had crashed from six million in 1984 to just one million in 1996. This was an appalling decline; the loss of five million penguins in 12 years, and it overlapped with the establishment of commercial fishing around the Falklands.

The Falkland Islands Government were very hostile towards my report, and I was told by Councillor Mike Summers and Chief Executive Andrew Gurr that such a report could be very damaging to the Falklands economy which depended on commercial fishing. I was asked to suppress my findings, but I refused, so the government simply dismissed my report. However when the evidence of a decline in Falklands penguins was shown to be conclusive, the government began blaming the problem on a world-wide decline in penguin numbers.

The penguins which had undergone the greatest declines were Southern Rockhopper and Magellanic penguins, and these were both restricted to the Falklands, Chile and Argentina. So for the government to suggest that the Falklands decline was part of a global trend meant that these penguins must also have declined in Chile and Argentina. At that time no such data existed to say whether this was true or not, so the only way to resolve the dilemma was to conduct a similar census in South America.

I decided that I would use the money I had put aside for the Falklands penguin census to conduct a similar census in Chile and Argentina, to determine whether the government's claim was true or not. To that end I flew to Punta Arenas to gather information from the University of Magellanes, CONAF, the Otway Foundation and the Patagonian Institute, about the location of known penguin colonies. I also approached the Chilean Navy in order to ask for help in getting to Isla Ildefonso and Diego Ramirez, which were two of the largest and remotest penguin colonies, since they had a naval weather station on these islands.

They were all very helpful and supportive of my project, and the Chilean Navy agreed to give me passage onboard one of the naval supply vessels which went to the islands every so often. The main problem would be matching the dates of their sailings with the time that I would have available to do the census. My priority still lay with the Seabird Monitoring Programme in the Falklands, which meant that I could not begin the South American penguin census until December 1996 when I would have free time.

My discussions with local naturalists made it apparent that the remote locations of many of the colonies around Chile and Argentina would make a land-based census, such as that conducted for the Falklands, almost impossible. The colonies were just too remote and spread over too large an area to make such a census feasible. I was forced to re-think my options and decided that a more realistic solution would be to conduct an aerial census. Clearly this would not be as accurate as a land-based census, but it was the only feasible option, and it did have the advantage of allowing a search for previously unrecorded sites, since even knowledge of colony locations was incomplete.

In order to evaluate the feasibility of such a plan, I travelled down to Ushuaia where much of the aerial census work around Tierra del Fuego would be based. My initial enquiries with the various agencies that did commercial flights were disappointing, because the cost was outrageously expensive. In order to fly such distances over open water they insisted on using a twin engine plane, such as a Twin Otter, which was very expensive. These planes also had fairly high stall-speeds, which would make photography and counting more difficult. I did however meet a local businessman called Ricardo Fernandez, who owned his own plane, and he told me that he was prepared to do the work at a competitive cost.

He owned a single-engine Cessna which he was prepared to use for the survey. He pointed out that flying long distances over open water was risky in a single-engine plane, but he said he was prepared to do it if I was. I was quite happy to run the risk, so we began putting together some proposals as to which areas I needed to cover. It soon became apparent that the flights were of such length that the Cessna lacked the necessary fuel range, however Ricardo assured me that he could overcome this problem by mounting additional fuel tanks inside the plane.

When I returned to Punta Arenas a few days later things were beginning to take shape, and what had at first seemed impossible was now beginning to seem possible. The main problem was still cost. Even using Ricardo instead of a commercial organisation, I still needed several weeks of flying to cover the enormous lengths of coastline involved, and that would not be cheap. Initial estimates were around £20,000 (US$30,000).

One way of reducing this cost was by using the Chilean Navy to reach the remotest islands of Ildefonso and Diego Ramirez. These were also by far the most risky to reach in a single-engined plane because they were such a long way from the mainland. Historical data suggested that these were the largest penguin colonies in South America, making them the slowest to count and adding to the problems of flight time. I therefore continued to seek passage onboard the Naval supply vessel.

Back in Punta Arenas I visited the Tercera Zona Naval headquarters to see if any progress had been made in getting a date for the passage. Unfortunately I was told that the dates were not set more than a couple of weeks in advance, so it would not be possible to find out until November whether or not the supply vessel would be sailing at a suitable time. This was leaving it rather late for my census which was due to commence in December.

On 9th July 1996, Falklands Conservation held a Committee Meeting, and I put forward my plans to carry out a penguin census in South America. I told them that I was proposing to fund the project myself, and did not need any financial support for the project. I did however invite them to participate to the extent of allowing me to do the census as part of my work time. I still had a large amount of holiday time owing and was prepared to use this time if needed, but I had rather hoped that they might consider the project sufficiently worthwhile to allow me to do it officially in work time.

After much consideration by the Committee members, I was told that they were very supportive of the project, but felt that work outside of the Falklands would have to be taken as holiday. I therefore reserved this time as annual leave.

CHAPTER THIRTEEN

By October 1996 plans for oil exploration were proceeding at a pace, and the Falklands was a buzz with anticipation. Falklands Conservation were approaching their Annual General Meeting, during which new trustees to govern the organisation were to be appointed by a vote of subscription paying members. Brian Summers had been an excellent Chairman for the organisation, but he was stepping down and a new chairman was to be appointed. Lewis Clifton, director of one of the companies about to drill for oil in the Falklands, put his name forward as a candidate.

I was horrified by the suggestion, and so were others. The Chairman held overall control of the organisation, and employees such as myself and my staff were obliged to abide by what the Chairman told us. I was greatly concerned by the conflict of interest that an oil company director would have with regard to environmental protection. I was convinced that the subscription paying members would not elect Clifton as Chairman at the Annual General Meeting, and I was not the only one. Other members shared my concern about Clifton's appointment.

To my astonishment the trustees then decided to ignore the democratic procedure laid down in the constitution, by electing themselves and Lewis Clifton into office prior to the Annual General Meeting. The appointments were presented to the Annual General Meeting after the event, without any alternative candidates being put forward. This was totally illegal, and in direct breach of the constitution and the very principals of democracy. The UK Charity Commission wrote to Falklands Conservation stating that they had breached the constitution, and that the appointments were illegal, but Falklands Conservation did not change their decision. The Falkland Islands' only wildlife conservation organisation was now in the hands of the director of Desire Petroleum, with dire consequences for Falklands wildlife.

On 9th October 1996 we held a meeting of the government advisory committee FENTAG (Falkland Islands Environmental Task Group). We had held several such meetings before, and made a number of suggestions to government about environmental protection that was required for oil exploration, but the Falkland Islands Government had disregarded virtually all of our suggestions. I made it clear at the meeting that I felt that government were not honouring their pledge to protect the environment, and that FENTAG was becoming nothing more than a rubber-stamp for government's disregard of environmental protection.

On numerous occasions the government had stated that plans for oil exploration were proceeding under the guidance of FENTAG, but in reality the advice of FENTAG was being ignored. I urged my fellow members of FENTAG to notify government that unless the environmental safety procedures which we had recommended were put in place, we would publicly dispute the Falkland Islands Government's statement that they were operating under our guidance. Within hours of the meeting, I received a phone call to tell me that an oil spill in the harbour had killed a number of cormorants.

I immediately went down to the port, known as FIPASS (Falklands Interim Port and Shipping Services), where sure enough oil had been discharged into the harbour by a moored vessel. The oil was lapping up against the walls of the very offices responsible for enforcing marine environmental protection. Amongst the oil were a number of dead cormorants, so I immediately returned to Stanley to notify the local press. They drove out with a photographer, who took photos of me pulling the dead birds out of the oil. Two days later the report made front page news, complete with photograph of oiled birds, but the harbour authorities still took no action.

The ship that had released the oil had been allowed to leave port without any charges being brought, and no serious attempt had been made to clean up the oil. The Harbour Authorities did not even have any equipment for dealing with spilt oil, and the Harbour Master had eventually gone to the local petrol station to see if they had anything to soak up oil. Four days later the oil had still not been cleaned up, and new cormorants were still being caught up in the oil. Port Authorities staff were forced to destroy the birds to put them out of their misery.

I protested strongly about the incident, and about the government's relaxed attitude towards environmental protection. I pointed out that if the Harbour Authorities could not prevent or clean up an oil spill that was lapping up against the walls of their own office, that they could hardly be trusted to control a major oil industry that would operate many miles out at sea. My complaints fell on deaf ears, and people within government began to express concern that a vocal environmentalist could spell trouble, and needed silencing.

First the Harbour Master called me, not to tell me that the oil had been cleaned up, but to say that I was no longer allowed to enter the Harbour facilities. Then Lewis Clifton called me to have lunch with him at the Malvina House Hotel, during which he severely reprimanded me for my comments about the oil spill. He told me that bad publicity could jeopardise the development of oil exploration, by enforcing unnecessary environmental constraints. I pointed out that it was my job as Conservation Officer to push for such environmental constraints.

Clifton responded by giving me a direct order as Chairman of the organisation that from now on Falklands Conservation staff, including myself, were not permitted to make any statements without first clearing them through him. The Falklands' only wildlife conservation organisation was now being officially censored by the director of the oil company that was about to start drilling for oil. Where in the world could such a thing happen except the Falklands?

A few days after the oil spill I flew to Punta Arenas to make the final arrangements for my South American penguin census. I discovered that there would not be a naval supply vessel going to Diego Ramirez during December or early January, which left aerial surveys as the only option. It was not too much of a disappointment, since I had rather expected it. In many ways it was simpler to organise the whole survey using the same method, rather than having to combine flights and navy vessels.

November was a busy month spent doing the usual nest counts of penguins, cormorants and albatross for Falklands Conservation. The work load had been increased again by the addition of two more study sites at Saunders Island and Port Stephens, but I still managed to complete the counts by the end of November with the help of my new assistant Carol Aldiss. With the annual monitoring work completed, I made my way back to Chile to turn my attention to the huge task which lay before me - the South American penguin census.

Many people I spoke to admired my dedication in attempting to carry out such a project, but thought I was crazy to spend £30,000 (US$45,000) of my own money doing it. In many ways they were probably right, and the project had become something of a personal obsession, but there was some logic behind it.

Having been recently diagnosed with two different types of cancer, I had little doubt that my days were numbered. Ever since my early childhood I had wanted to achieve something of real merit in the protection of God's creatures. I could think of no better opportunity than this. With the world's Southern Rockhopper penguin population being restricted to Chile, Argentina and the Falklands, this was a one-off opportunity to complete a world census, and to compare populations in South America with the Falkland Islands which had been censused the previous year. With no other sources of funding available, I either paid for the work myself, or lost the chance to accomplish a life-long ambition.

From Punta Arenas I took the bus to Ushuaia, where I met up with Ricardo. As promised the plane had been prepared for the census work. All the passenger seats had been removed to make way for a row of 200 litre drums, which were necessary to reach the more distant islands. Each time the plane's main fuel tank began running low, I had to manually pump fuel from one of the 200 litre drums into the main fuel tank to refill it. The whole plane stank of fuel when I did this, and I am sure it would never have passed any safety inspection, but it worked.

From Ushuaia we began surveying the area from Isla de los Estados to Cape Horn. This was a vast area to cover, but we had already determined which areas held suitable coastline for penguins. Even so, the distances of ocean to be crossed by a single-engine plane were vast. With only one engine, any mechanical breakdown would have meant almost certain death. Even if one survived the crash, the survival time for being immersed in such cold water was minutes, with no prospect of rescue for hours or even days.

A larger plane with two motors would have been able to cover the vast open areas of ocean much faster, but the advantage of our small plane soon became apparent. Once we located each of the penguin colonies, we were able to make our approach directly into the prevailing wind, allowing us to reduce our ground speed to the point where on many occasions we were almost stationary. This was perfect for providing a steady platform from which to do my counts and take photos. A faster plane would have flown over the colony too quickly to have given me time to do the counts.

We were usually able to fly low enough that I was able to see the birds clearly without the need for binoculars, making counting a lot easier than I had anticipated. Indeed, by looking down on the colony from above at such close range, it was easier than doing the counts from the ground. I also took photographs which were of sufficient clarity as to allow individual birds to be counted, allowing a cross-reference with the counts I had made during the fly-over. I recorded all my counts and comments on audio tape as I did them, which meant that I did not need to be distracted by writing things down.

From Ushuaia we moved across to Puerto Williams, enabling us to cover the area from Diego Ramirez to Isla Noir. Despite flying from dawn to dusk, seven days a week, we were gradually falling behind schedule as a result of the huge distances to be covered. By the time we were ready to concentrate on the huge length of coastline north of Isla Noir, it was clear that we could not cover all the area in the time remaining.

Fortunately, prior to leaving Puerto Williams we met another pilot called Toni Silva, who was also flying north on his way to Peru. He was using a twin-engine King Air, and offered to help. We sent him home via a route that would cover coastline which had no known colonies, enabling him to confirm that these unexplored areas were empty. Toni would notify us upon his arrival in Peru as to whether or not he had found any colonies. If he did, he would relay their position so that we could conduct a count. This enabled Ricardo and I to concentrate on the more promising areas, which saved us a huge amount of time.

This encounter proved to be very fortunate indeed, since the area of coastline north of Isla Noir was virtually devoid of penguins. There were just a handful of tiny colonies separated by hundreds of kilometres, and we did not find any colonies in this area that had not already been reported. It was no surprise when Toni confirmed that he had not seen any colonies on the route he had taken.

After two months of flying we were both absolutely exhausted. I left Ricardo in Punta Arenas where he planned to crash out for a week before returning home. I flew straight back to the Falklands to begin the second phase of my seabird monitoring work for Falklands Conservation.

I was immediately faced with a number of problems which nobody had been able to resolve in my absence. Our field assistant, Carol, had been taken ill by a flu bug and was unfit for work. Jeremy Smith, whom I was relying on to conduct chick counts around East Falkland with Carol, had refused to work on his own, so nothing had been done. I immediately found a replacement assistant, and the fieldwork got underway, albeit a few days behind schedule. Jeremy set off to cover East Falkland, whilst I flew out to Saunders Island and Port Stephens on my own.

I also discovered from the Customs & Immigration Department that my application for residency permit had been turned down. The usual requirements for such a permit were a clean police record, secure finances, and a medical examination, all of which had been favourable. I could not see any justifiable reason for being refused, and suspected it was because of my calls for wildlife protection against oil exploration and commercial fishing, so I asked them for the grounds of the refusal. They refused to tell me the grounds.

I took legal advice on the matter, and was informed that it was a violation of International Law for the grounds of my refusal to be withheld. The Attorney General, David Lang, confirmed that the Immigration Department was obliged by law to give me the reason, but they still refused to do so.

On 22nd February 1997 I flew to Quito in Ecuador to attend a Birdlife International conference. I stopped off for a couple of days in Punta Arenas on route, in order to collect my aerial photographs from the penguin census work. Whilst I was there I met a young lady called Elena, who worked for Corcoran Ltd, the largest import and export company in Punta Arenas. We got on really well together during our first date, and I asked to see her again when I returned to Punta Arenas.

When I checked in at the terminal in Santiago for my flight to Quito, I was told that I could not go on board with two items of hand luggage. I either had to check in one of the bags, or not go, so I had no choice. When I arrived in Quito, the bag which I had checked in had been opened and several items stolen. Apparently it was a common scam to make people check in one of their bags and then stealing from it, knowing that most people keep items of value in bags they want to keep onboard.

Birdlife International had promised that a representative would be waiting for me at the airport, but there was nobody around. I was therefore forced to take a taxi to find a hotel, since Birdlife International had given me no out of hours contact number. The following day was a Sunday, so again I could not get in touch with Birdlife International to find out what was happening or where I was supposed to go. I decided to take a stroll around the city, and came across an open air market.

After a few minutes in the market, I was jostled from behind, and pushed into a young man standing in front of me. I apologised to him and stepped back. As I did so the same thing happened again, only this time I saw him slice open my breast pocket with a cut-throat razor and make a grab for my wallet. Fearing that he might use the razor as a weapon, I punched him as hard as I could in the face, causing him to drop to the ground. I turned round to see who was behind me, but with so many people it was impossible to tell who had been his accomplice.

I turned back to face the first thief, and it was clear that he was badly hurt from the blow I had given him. Blood was pouring from the man's nose, as he writhed about on the floor in pain. Several people were looking at me as though I had provoked the attack, so I decided it was time to leave. If nobody had witnessed the attempt to steal my wallet, I did not really want to wait around to explain to the police why I had hit the man so hard.

I made my way through the crowd to an open area where I could take a proper look at what they had done.

My jacket pocket had two large slashes across it, and so did my wallet. Even the bank notes inside my wallet had been cut clean in half by the razor. It must have been very sharp, and I was lucky that they had only cut my jacket and wallet.

The following day I finally made contact with Birdlife International, who apologised for having failed to meet me at the airport. I joined all the other participants, and we were taken by bus to a conference centre about 30 kilometres from Quito. The conference itself went well, but the Birdlife International administration continued to be a shambles.

For whatever reason, the Birdlife International staff requested that everybody hand over their return air tickets to reception, so that they could make the necessary confirmations as a group. Towards the end of the week we were given our tickets back, and all seemed well. On the very last day I was having my lunch, just a couple of hours before the coach was due to take us back to the airport, when one of the Birdlife International members of staff came over to me and informed me that there was a problem.

Birdlife had somehow forgotten to make my flight confirmation, and as a result my return passage had been cancelled. My seat had been resold, and I was stranded. I was not pleased, and asked what they intended to do about it. Birdlife International's solution to the problem they had created was to drop me off at the nearest travel agents in Quito, where I was left to sort out the mess on my own. I left the conference with the impression that Birdlife International could not be trusted to organise the care of a pet parrot, let alone endangered species.

As a result of missing my scheduled flight from Quito, I missed my connection with the weekly flight back to the Falklands. I therefore returned to Punta Arenas and spent a few more days with Elena whilst I waited for the next flight. Elena had a few days of holiday owing, so we went to Puerto Natales and Torres del Paine where we got to know each other better.

Back in the Falklands there was great discussion amongst Falklands Conservation staff about a book being written by UK trustee, Robin Woods. The book was to be produced by Falklands Conservation, and called the *"Atlas of Breeding Birds of the Falkland Islands"*. It included population totals for each bird in the Falklands - totals which were based on nothing more than questionnaires sent out to farmers. Robin Woods had asked farmers to fill in questionnaires stating how many of each bird species lived on their 50,000 hectares of land, and then published these numbers as though they were real census data.

Farmers in the Falklands are very knowledgeable about the wildlife around them, and can provide a wealth of information, but nobody can say how many of each species of bird live in 50,000 hectares of farmland without spending weeks doing bird census work. The population figures in the Atlas of Breeding Birds were wrong for every single species for which genuine population data were available. Worst still was the penguin section, which gave population figures that were approximately double what we had just recorded during our own penguin census.

Our penguin census of the Falklands had revealed huge population declines. It had been suggested by the Falkland Islands Government that these declines were part of a global trend, but my census of South America had shown that this was not the case. The penguin decline was only occurring in the Falklands, not in nearby South America. This needed urgent investigation, but the false population figures given in the Atlas of Breeding Birds made it look as though penguin populations had not undergone such a dramatic decline.

I immediately raised the question as to why Falklands Conservation would support the publication of population figures which they knew to be false? Why would figures from somebody who had conducted their census from a desk, take precedence over a census that had employed over a hundred field operatives? Why would Falklands Conservation wish to mislead people into thinking that penguin populations were higher than they really were? I could think of only one answer - to hide the truth, and to allow oil exploration and commercial fishing to continue unhindered.

On 31st March 1997 we held a committee meeting, and I raised the matter with the trustees. I told the committee that if Falklands Conservation supported a publication stating there to be twice as many penguins as actually recorded by their own census, that they were not only being dishonest, but were also weakening the argument for environmental protection for the forthcoming oil exploration. Several trustees agreed with my view, and it was postponed for further discussion. Lewis Clifton was furious.

ince being ordered by Clifton to do so, but I
was not prepared to falsify research data in order to
hide a collapse in penguin populations. I reminded
him that it was Falklands Conservation's duty to report
the findings we made, not to cover them up so that
oil exploration and commercial fishing could proceed
unhindered.

Clifton warned me that if I didn't stop going against
government policy, that he would see to it personally
that I was kicked out of Falklands Conservation, kicked
off all the environmental committees, and booted out
of the Falklands as an undesirable.

I replied that I did not believe that other people
within Falklands Conservation and government would
let him abuse his power in such a manner. I really
thought that honest people would speak out if such
things happened. How wrong I was. In November
2003 the Supreme Court of the Falkland Islands would
find the Governor, Attorney General, Chief Executive
and elected members of Executive Council, guilty of

human rights abuse against me, after all the threats Clifton made this day had come to fruition.

Clifton moved to the doorway without speaking. He turned around and pointed his finger at me like a pistol, before finally leaving. I knew then that I would have to watch my back.

I began to feel quite shaky about what had happened, and instead of going straight home I made myself a coffee and sat down. I began to regret taking such a bold stance, after all I knew Clifton's reputation. But quite honestly the alternative was unspeakable. I was a conservationist because I believed in what I was doing. I believe that mankind acts as guardian of God's creation, and was insulted by the suggestion that I would sell my principals for a large pay rise. It was a while since I had prayed to God, but I still believed that I was doing His will by protecting the beauty that He had created in the world.

There was no way that I could have brought myself to falsify research data in exchange for job security and a pay rise. It seemed quite apparent to me that as Director of Desire Petroleum, Clifton was more interested in keeping the oil exploration process on track, than he was about conservation. If somebody wanted to cripple an environmental organisation, there was no better way of doing it than by becoming Chairman. I knew in my heart that I had done the right thing, but I had more difficulty convincing myself that I had done the wise thing.

I decided to confront the problem head on, and the following day I told everybody in the office about the threats their Chairman had made. Nobody was the least bit surprised, and their only comment was that I should watch my back.

The following day I flew to Punta Arenas again, this time to represent the Falklands at another conference being held at the University of Magellanes. Since the conference was held in Punta Arenas, I was also able to spend time with Elena, and our relationship began to get serious.

On 24th April I attended the very first Falkland Islands Environmental Oil Forum meeting, which was a body aimed at co-ordinating the efforts of oil companies and environmentalists in order to protect the environment. The meeting was held in a very positive spirit, and it appeared as though the oil company representatives were eager to employ sound environmental practices. Indeed a number of the representatives expressed concern that the Falkland Islands Government were the ones who seemed reluctant to introduce environmental protection.

During the meeting I put together proposals for a couple of environmental monitoring projects, one being a seabirds at sea study, and the other a penguin satellite tagging programme. Both would investigate seabird distribution at sea, which was important during oil exploration. Both projects were greeted with great enthusiasm, and it was generally felt by the oil company representatives that funding could be made available to undertake these projects.

In addition to the projects I presented to the Environmental Oil Forum, I also presented two additional projects to the Falkland Islands Government for funding. One was a baseline survey of wetland sites, to evaluate their potential for designation under the RAMSAR convention. The other was an island-wide census of Striated Caracara, to be carried out along the lines of the highly successful penguin census. Both projects required somebody with training in biological surveying, but since I was a qualified Biological Surveyor, I was able to keep the projected costs low.

I had two motives for keeping costs low. The first was that by keeping costs low there was a much greater likelihood that the committee would agree to fund the project. The second was that I suspected that Lewis Clifton was indeed going to try and kick me out of Falklands Conservation. As the only qualified Biological Surveyor in the Falklands, I knew that Falklands Conservation would be unable to complete these projects at such a low cost without me.

A couple of days later the office computer broke down. Working on such a tight budget we had no funds to purchase another computer, so I brought down my own desktop computer to put in its place. I still had my own laptop computer, so I was able to manage without it.

My concerns about my future employment were borne out when I was told that my job was being re-advertised, and that Lewis Clifton would be in charge of the recruitment process. On the 20th May we had a committee meeting, during which the recruitment procedure was outlined by Clifton.

In early June 1997 we received the news that the Falkland Islands Government had increased Falklands Conservation's annual budget to £125,000, a four-fold increase on their previous funding. To most people in the organisation this looked like a pay off for keeping oil exploration on track under Clifton's leadership. Since I had made it clear that I would have no part of it, I knew this signalled that I was to be kicked out.

I was called into hospital for a biopsy of the large intestine, to determine whether pains I was getting could indicate a return of my cancer. I notified Lewis Clifton that I would be in hospital undergoing surgery on 17th June, and that I would therefore be unable to attend an interview on that day. Three days later, Clifton notified me that the interviews had been set on the exact day of my operation. He told me that if I did not attend, I would not be eligible for re-employment.

I thought about cancelling my operation, but I was frightened by the prospect that my cancer might have returned, and that cancelling my surgery could have potentially fatal consequences. I took a taxi to the hospital at 8am, and was taken into theatre around noon.

I woke up from general anaesthetic early afternoon feeling slightly groggy, but otherwise not too bad. I looked at my watch to see if I still had time to attend the interview and I did, so I got out of bed and started getting dressed. One of the nurses asked me what I was doing, and I explained that if I did not attend the interview I would loose my job. She said that she did not believe that an employer would dismiss me on the grounds that I had been in hospital undergoing surgery during my interview. I assured her that this particular employer would.

I took a taxi home, changed into my suit, and got to the interview with several minutes to spare. As I waited outside the door to be called, I felt distinctly unwell. The pain which an hour before had been just a niggle, had now spread up through my abdomen, and had become intolerable. I felt cold and clammy, as though the blood was draining out of my body.

I was finally called into the interview room, and asked to sit down. As expected the interview panel was headed by Lewis Clifton, who opened by asking me what I thought I could offer the organisation. I replied that I had achieved a huge amount since joining the organisation. I had created and developed the computer system which Falklands Conservation now used. Prior to my appointment letters had been done on a typewriter, and data had been stored on scraps of notepaper.

On the research side I had expanded the seabird monitoring programme from 3 species at 3 sites, to 7 species at 8 sites, and this increase had been the result of improved efficiency, since no additional funds had been assigned to the fieldwork. I had also planned and executed an island-wide penguin census, which had been a tremendous success: a hugely ambitious project which had been considered impossible by many, but which had been completed without a hitch.

With regard to future projects, I pointed out that I was a qualified and experienced biological surveyor, skills which were essential in carrying out the forthcoming RAMSAR and Striated Caracara surveys. I became aware that I was sounding boastful, but I wanted to remind the interview panel that I held skills and qualifications which were valuable to the organisation's success.

Clifton then asked me why they should re-employ me when I had shown disloyalty to the organisation. I asked him to explain what disloyalty he was referring to, and he told me that I had been seeking alternative employment behind their backs. He said that people within Falklands Conservation sat on other committees, and had become aware of my other job applications.

In all the years that I had been with Falklands Conservation, I had only ever applied for one other job. Far from doing this behind Falklands Conservation's back, the Chairman at that time, Brian Summers, had not only been informed, but had agreed to give me a reference for my application.

The application had been a shambles in actual fact. Several weeks after applying I heard that Jeremy Smith's wife had been given the job, and that she had been the only candidate. I contacted the Human Resources Department to find out how she could have been the only candidate when I had also applied. I was told that my application had been accidentally over-looked. I was told they were very sorry, but that it was too late to do anything about it.

I assured Clifton that this was the only job I had ever applied for, and asked him what other jobs he thought I had applied for. He said that he did not intend to discuss the matter, and that the interview was at an end. I left feeling very disappointed. It was obvious that Clifton was indeed trying to kick me out, just as he had threatened. My only hope was that other people on the panel were strong enough to stand up against him, and ask him for details of the accusations he had made so they could verify their validity.

By the time I got home I discovered that I was passing blood. I still felt cold and clammy, and now I felt really weak. The pain inside my abdomen was unbearable, and I took 4 paracetamol tablets to take the edge off it. I lay down on the bed to try and ease the pain, and the next thing I knew it was morning.

I had lain on the bed for some 15 hours. The pain had eased off, but I felt terribly weak. I staggered to my feet and tried to make my way to the kitchen to make a coffee, but I never got there. I passed out in the corridor, and the next thing I knew I was being rushed to hospital in an ambulance.

I felt very embarrassed at being taken into hospital by ambulance. There was no denying that it had been my own stupid fault for ignoring the doctor's advice, but the interview had been so important to me. As it was I now regretted ever going to the interview. It would have been better to let Clifton kick me out for being in hospital at the time of the interview.

In the evening Jeremy Smith came to see how I was. I told him about the interview, and he told me not to worry. He assured me that he had only ever heard positive things said about my work by other trustees, and that there were no other candidates with the necessary qualifications or experience to do the research work. That was partly what worried me. I knew that without staff qualified in biological surveying and bird census techniques, the standard of research would be diminished, which would suit Clifton and certain other people. With no scientific credibility, the Falkland Islands Government would be able to continue unhindered with oil exploration and commercial fishing.

After two more days in hospital I was allowed home, and on the 23rd of June we held a committee meeting, but there was still no news about my job. The following morning I went into work and there was a letter on my desk from Lewis Clifton. It contained the news that I had expected. My job had been given to somebody else, and my employment with Falklands Conservation was to be terminated that very week.

When later asked by reporters why I had been dismissed, Lewis Clifton stated on record to the Guardian newspaper that Falklands Conservation "*had decided to structure the organisation on a different footing since they were concerned about the level of publicity oiled birds were getting. There was concern that Bingham was a bit of a loose canon*". (The Guardian 12th October 1999).

To me this was an astonishing statement for Clifton to make, especially to the press. It had clearly been the duty of both myself as Conservation Officer, and Falklands Conservation as a whole, to draw attention to the oiling of seabirds and the decline in penguin numbers. To state that I had been dismissed for drawing attention to oiled birds demonstrated just how much Falklands Conservation had been crippled by people with financial interests in oil exploration and commercial fishing. Lewis Clifton's statement demonstrated how Falklands Conservation had reduced the number of references to oiled birds through censorship, rather than through higher standards of environmental protection.

I was given just two days notice to remove my personal belongings, and to prepare what I could for my successor. I contacted Clifton and some of the other trustees and suggested that I be given more time before leaving. This would not only allow me the opportunity to look for new employment, and to seek a residency permit, but also time to work with my successor to show them the ropes. I was very concerned that if my successor took over after I had already left, that they would not understand the research methodology, the computer databases, or the Geographic Information System. Another problem was that Falklands Conservation were still using my computer, which would have to be removed when I left. Clifton told me that it was all in hand, and refused my request to extend the two days notice I had been given.

As I was hurriedly packing away my personal belongings, Nicki Buxton called over with a new computer which Clifton had ordered for the office. Unfortunately she did not have the necessary software to set up the computer. She had ordered the software from Britain, but it was not due to arrive until after I had left. The only solution was to copy the database into a directory, where it would remain until the necessary software arrived to open it. I wrote down the details of how to open the database when the software arrived, and said my farewells.

I contacted the Immigration Department for a temporary residency permit in order to put my things in order. Without it I would have been deported from the Falklands upon termination of my employment with Falklands Conservation. I could not help thinking that the very short notice I had been given by Falklands Conservation was so as to force me to leave the Falklands in just such a manner. Two days was a disgracefully short amount of notice after nearly 4 years of service.

The Immigration Department agreed to give me a 3 month permit, which gave me time to make new plans before being forced to leave, so I went to Punta Arenas and spent six weeks with Elena whilst I thought out my strategy. She was the one person who could cheer me up after all that had happened.

CHAPTER FOURTEEN

As soon as I returned from my 6 weeks in Chile, I contacted a solicitor to set up a privately registered company, so that I could continue my wildlife research as a private consultant. I also began trying for other types of employment, especially government jobs which came with automatic residency status. One such job was Power Station Operator with the Public Works Department.

I also wrote to Falklands Conservation offering my services for the two research projects which government had agreed to fund. I knew that there was nobody else in the Falklands with biological surveying and bird census training, and that acquiring overseas specialists trained in such skills would push the costs way above the budget that they had been allocated.

I offered to do these projects under sub-contract for substantially less than the Falkland Islands Government were paying Falklands Conservation. This meant that I would have assumed full responsibility for completing the project within budget, and Falklands Conservation would have been left with a profit from what the Falkland Islands Government paid them. I also suggested that if this was not acceptable, I would be equally willing to work as an assistant on a normal wage arrangement.

Falklands Conservation never even acknowledged my letters, but my replacement, Becky Ingham, told me informally that Clifton had dismissed the idea out of hand. This left Falklands Conservation with an enormous problem.

A desk study conducted several years before had identified a number of potential candidate sites for designation under the RAMSAR convention. I had therefore applied to the Falkland Islands Government for funding to conduct baseline surveys of the four most promising candidates. With no other qualified biological surveyor in the Falklands, this left Falklands Conservation with the choice of either abandoning the project, or employing a baseline surveyor from Britain at great expense.

Falklands Conservation did neither. Instead they claimed the money from the Falkland Islands Government, and then wrote a 'desk study' - a general report which merely redrafted the work that had already been done in the past. Not surprisingly this 'desk study' concluded with the recommendation that a baseline survey of candidate sites was needed, the very work which was supposed to have been carried out with the funds they had been given!

The other project was the Striated Caracara census, which required even more specialist skills. It needed a researcher with raptor census training to lead the census, but at such short notice it was impossible to find a replacement Biological Surveyor. Falklands Conservation eventually decided to employ one of their trustees, Robin Woods of 'Atlas of Breeding Birds' fame. Robin Woods is the only person I know who can accurately determine the population of birds simply by sending out questionnaires to land owners (see *Atlas of Breeding Birds of the Falkland Islands*). Clearly all the Biological Surveyors in the world, who spend years studying bird populations to produce such data, have all got it wrong. All they needed to do was send out questionnaires!

Having said that, Robin Woods is without doubt one of the leading authorities on Falklands bird identification and behaviour, but a bird census does not require such skills, it requires a person qualified in bird census methodology. Conducting a bird census is like doing a stock-take: it is counting the number of birds in the population, just like a stock-take counts the number of books on a shelf. One does not need a degree in literature to do a stock-take in a bookshop, but one does need stock-taking experience. Stock-taking of bird populations requires special training, which is why courses in Biological Surveying were devised.

Falklands Conservation advertised for a field assistant to help with the project. This was basically somebody to help carry the bags, and the wage was just £40 per week, but I swallowed my pride and applied for the job. Needless to say I did not even get an acknowledgement of my application.

With nobody qualified in bird census techniques, Falklands Conservation devised a totally inappropriate methodology which attempted to count territories. This not only gives incorrect results for birds such as caracaras, but is also very time consuming, and not surprisingly the census ran out of time and funding with only half the work done. With only half the breeding sites counted, using faulty methodology, it was impossible to produce the population total that had been the sole purpose of the project.

Because of the importance of the project, Falklands Conservation were forced to apply for new funding to repeat the project again the following year, wasting over £20,000 (US$30,000) of tax-payers money.

Falklands Conservation's penguin research was also breaking down in a similar manner. Falklands Conservation's own newsletter reported Becky Ingham and Andrea Clausen taking a trip to count Rockhoppers in late October, unaware that population counts cannot begin until the end of egg-laying, which for Rockhoppers meant mid-November. Late October was okay for Gentoo and Magellanic penguins, but not for Rockhoppers which lay eggs later. Falklands Conservation's annual report then recorded a breeding success of 1.2 chicks per nest for a species that only rears one egg! They had accidentally mistaken moulting juveniles for chicks when they did the chick count.

Realising that they were out of their depth, Andrea Clausen of Falklands Conservation wrote to me saying:

"Hi Mike. I have just been working up the Breeding Pair numbers for the various sites monitored this season and was wondering if you could give me a pointer. As you may recall I told you I had problems counting the Breeding Pairs. Well I did some density measurements and tried to roughly work out the population - unfortunately I don't think this has been very successful! I would really appreciate your comments and numbers."

As requested I gave Falklands Conservation the numbers from my own Environmental Research Unit studies, and explained the correct techniques for conducting population counts, but the underline problem was more difficult to resolve. Falklands Conservation's trustees were sacrificing the organisation's scientific integrity for political and personal motives, and other members of the organisation were of the same opinion. One such member, Mark Nedd, put my name forward for election as a trustee at the 1997 Annual General Meeting. According to Charity Law and Falklands Conservation's own Constitution, once a name was proposed and seconded, they were under a legal obligation to put that name forward to the members for a vote at the Annual General Meeting, so that members could select their chosen representatives in a democratic manner. Of course this did not happen.

Falklands Conservation's Board of Trustees acted in a totally illegal manner by re-electing themselves prior to the Annual General Meeting, and removing my name from the list of candidates presented to the Annual General Meeting, making it look as though no other candidates were standing for election. This denied the members of the organisation their democratic right to vote. Several members complained that this had been done to prevent me being elected as a Trustee, where I could have kept an eye on the standard of scientific research being carried out, and the matter was reported to the Charity Commission.

The Charity Commission investigated and confirmed that Falklands Conservation had acted in an illegal and unconstitutional manner. They informed Falklands Conservation that the appointments made were illegal and invalid, including the appointment of Lewis Clifton as Chairman. But as is so often the case in the Falklands, Falklands Conservation ignored the ruling, and made no effort to rectify the matter. With the Falklands being so remote, and under independent law, it is impossible for organisations such as the Charity Commission and Police Complaints Authority to prosecute or enforce rulings made under British law. The trustees who had been illegally elected to positions of power in Falklands Conservation remained in office with the Falkland Islands Government's full support.

Despite my lack of success with Falklands Conservation, I fared well in my attempts to rebuild my life. I had established myself as an independent researcher under the name of the Environmental Research Unit, and had been offered the post of Power Station Operator, which being a government post gave me automatic residency rights.

I had had my name down for a building plot since 1994, and the large number of plots now being made available on the new East Stanley Development meant that I was finally offered one. I began designing my house and submitted building plans, which were approved by the building committee. Unfortunately the plot itself was not yet ready for release, so I could not actually get started with the building work.

My work in the power station was pretty much what I had expected. Most of the time the Power Station Operator was just on hand to ensure that everything was running smoothly. Each hour they would go around the generators and write down the meter readings, to ensure that everything was okay. As the load increased and decreased during the course of the day, the operators also changed the number and size of generators to keep in line with demand.

Each operator worked on his own, most of the time being spent sitting in the control room doing his own thing, whilst keeping an eye on the meter readings. Other operators read the newspaper, listened to the radio, practised the guitar or even made craft items. Generally speaking the more occupied a person was, the more alert they would remain. Sitting watching the clock was not only boring, but led to people feeling tired and even falling asleep, especially during the night shift. The best thing was to keep busy.

I still had my laptop computer, so I began taking this into work each day. During my spare time I would write letters, do accounts, and even write articles and manuscripts. With the Environmental Research Unit now officially established, I wrote up the results of the Falkland Islands and South American penguin censuses, and sent the manuscripts away for publication to *Penguin Conservation* magazine, and *Oryx*, the peer-reviewed scientific journal of Fauna and Flora International.

As a matter of courtesy, I notified Falklands Conservation that I was publishing the articles, and explained that I would be including the results of the Falkland Islands Penguin Census. It is a general rule that confidential results gathered whilst in the employment of an organisation remain the property of that organisation, until they are put into the public domain. The results of the Falkland Islands Penguin Census had officially been put into the public domain, even though they had not been widely circulated for political reasons. This gave me a legal right to use the data in my publications.

The articles I had written were aimed at widely publishing the penguin census data for both the Falklands and South America. By now the Atlas of Breeding Birds had been published, and the articles I was about to publish would show that the Atlas was using penguin population figures which were double those which Falklands Conservation themselves had counted. It came as no surprise when my publishers received a letter from Dr John Croxall, Falklands Conservation's UK Chairman, trying to block the publication, and threatening legal action if the Falkland Islands Penguin Census data was made public.

My publishers and I had lengthy discussions on the matter, and having taken legal advice we were convinced that Falklands Conservation had no legal right to suppress the data. The manuscripts were therefore published.

Falklands Conservation´s own census data was now available for comparison with the data presented in their "*Atlas of Breeding Birds of the Falkland Islands*". Falklands Conservation's own census, which I had led, recorded 297,000 breeding pairs of Rockhopper penguins, but their Atlas of Breeding Birds quoted 550,000 breeding pairs. Similarly the census had recorded 65,000 breeding pairs of Gentoo penguins, but their Atlas of Breeding Birds quoted 102,000 breeding pairs. Faced with questions from concerned members of the public, Falklands Conservation were forced to admit that the census figures published in *Oryx* and *Penguin Conservation* were correct, but offered no explanation as to why figures approximately double those of the census had been published in the Atlas.

The correct figures would have placed greater emphasis on providing stronger environmental protection, but by the time my articles were finally published, oil exploration was already underway. Within weeks of the first oil rig arriving in the Falklands, three separate oil spills occurred killing and contaminating hundreds of penguins, cormorants and other wildlife. To say "I told you so" gave me no pleasure at all. Indeed it was a personal failure for me that this had been allowed to occur. I had warned so many people that oiled penguins would result if an oil company director ran the Falklands' only wildlife conservation organisation, and now it had become a reality.

I had stated on many occasions that wildlife conservation had been sold out to people with ulterior motives, people who had crippled Falklands Conservation from within. I now felt that the evidence was there for all to see, not only because of what had happened, but because of the way that Falklands Conservation now ran to the defence of government and oil companies in the face of dying penguins.

Falklands Conservation immediately claimed that the spilt oil had come from outside the Falkland's 300 kilometre conservation zone, clearing the Falkland Islands Government of any blame. This was despite the fact that the Gentoo penguins and cormorants caught up in the oil were known to forage less than 30 kilometres from shore, making it impossible for them to have become contaminated by oil outside Falklands waters. A FIGAS aircraft later spotted the third and final oil slick, confirming that it had indeed occurred well within Falklands' waters, contrary to what Falklands Conservation had claimed.

The oil spills had not come from the drilling rig, but had been discharged by oil rig supply vessels. Such blatant disregard for the environment was a direct result of the Falkland Islands Government's refusal to instigate minimum standards of environmental protection, and Falklands Conservation's decision to accept government money in exchange for turning a blind eye to environmental damage. As Lewis Clifton had stated in The Guardian, Falklands Conservation had indeed reduced the number of references to oiled birds, but by employing staff willing to keep quiet rather than by carrying out any actual conservation work. The actual number of oiled birds had escalated, and now even the public became outraged.

It became apparent to most people that Falklands Conservation were doing a better job of protecting private investments in oil exploration and commercial fishing, than of protecting wildlife. They had published false data, attempted to suppress reports of penguin declines, blamed the oil spills on anyone except the Falklands government, and appointed directors of oil, fishing and shipping companies onto the board of trustees by illegal means.

As drilling operations were drawing to a close, no commercially viable quantities of oil had been found, barely enough to cover a coastline of penguins in fact. It was looking bleak for those who had invested heavily in the venture, but then suddenly came unofficial rumours of a major oil strike. Desire Petroleum share prices shot up, and then as they peaked, came the announcement that it had been a hoax. No oil had been found after all. Of course share prices tumbled, but not before investors in Falklands oil had made a killing from the massive increase in share prices. Not bad for investors in an oil venture that failed.

I had done an excellent job of revealing the corruption within Falklands Conservation, but a very poor job of getting people to accept the environmental protection that was needed. The number of dead penguins caught up in the oil spills was testimony to my personal failure in that respect. I had also made myself a number of powerful enemies, and so the dirty war began.

One of the trustees, Mike Morrison, mentioned to me that trustees within Falklands Conservation had begun accusing me of destroying their database. When

I asked what reason they had for thinking this, he told me that they had been unable to get the database up and running since I had left the previous June. I offered to go into the office and sort it out, and I soon discovered the problem.

What had been left on the computer as a database file had been converted into a word processor file, scrambling all the data. No back up had been made by the person responsible. The computer records clearly showed that this had happened more than a month after I had finished my employment with Falklands Conservation. I had actually been in Chile on the date that the file had been corrupted, so even Falklands Conservation were forced to concede that it was not my fault.

I later discovered that the computer had undergone a series of crashes due to a faulty power supply provided by Nicki Buxton, which is why it had taken so long for the problem to come to light. Even so, it seemed unlikely that this could have caused the loss of data. It was far more likely that somebody without experience of databases had opened the Microsoft Works file in word processor mode, and accidentally saved it in word processor format.

I printed out the file information as proof that the database had been corrupted more than a month after I had left their employment. I offered to try restoring the data using data recovery software, but Falklands Conservation declined my offer. Having proven that my successor had corrupted the data more than a month after my departure, I assumed that it would be the end of the matter, but I was wrong.

My building plot finally became available, and I began digging the holes for the foundations by hand. Each pit was about half a cubic metre in volume, and took about 2 hours to dig. I was still doing shift work at the power station, so the amount of time I had available depended on what shift I was on. On average I was able to spend about 3 to 4 hours per day working on the house.

With the holes for the foundations now dug, I hired metal casings to mould the piles which the house would sit on, and these were then filled with concrete. I did not have a fancy laser-sight to get the piles level, as most builders would use, so instead I used a plastic hose pipe full of water. Water always keeps the same level at both ends of the hose pipe, so this enabled me to get the levels exactly right.

Then I purchased 275mm x 50mm beams and bolted them together in pairs across the rows of piles. Cross joists were then laid across these double beams forming the basis of the floor. I constructed the walls from 100mm x 50mm timber frames, which I made up as I went along. Six weeks after digging the first hole, I had completed the basic framework of the house except for the roof, and I had done all the work myself

The roof was about the hardest challenge. It was to be made out of large w-braced roof trusses, which I designed and assembled on the ground using lengths of 100mm x 50mm timber. I constructed a jig to ensure that all the trusses were identical, and spent about two weeks cutting the timbers and making up the trusses. When they were complete, I was faced with the task of getting them up onto the top of the walls by myself.

Each truss was 10 metres long and weighed 40 kilograms, and I had to lift them onto the top of the walls which were about 3 metres above ground level. I achieved this by hanging the trusses upside down inside the house, supported at each end by the outer walls, like a giant letter "V". Of course the trusses needed to be turned over to form the frame for the roof, so I made up a large T-shaped pole which I used to push the truss up and over.

At first I had to lay a piece of wood against the gable end to support the first truss, otherwise it would have fallen off the end of the building when I flipped it over. Once the first truss was up and nailed into place, I was then able to turn each truss over in turn so that it leaned against the previous one. One by one I lifted each truss on to the walls, and flipped it over to make the framework for the roof. I felt incredibly pleased with my achievement. My sense of achievement was reinforced every time people commented that I couldn't possibly have lifted them up on my own.

Once the framework was up and fully braced, the walls and roof were ready for panelling. This was not difficult, but needed a lot of stamina because of the size of the sheets which I needed to lift up single-handed. Day by day, and sheet by sheet, the house was panelled over, and by mid-winter I had finally got the house closed in so that I could work under cover during bad weather.

With secure employment and a house of my own, I resubmitted my application for Permanent Residency Permit, which would have entitled me to remain in the Falklands without my government job in the Power

Station. I had also been able to conduct a series of coastline sensitivity surveys which I felt were vital in view of the existing oil exploration. The Environmental Planning Department heard about the coastline surveys I had performed, and in March 1998 they wrote to me asking if I would be prepared to sell them the data I had gathered.

I replied that I did not require payment for the work I had already done, but that I was seeking funding in order to complete the work. I told the Environmental Planning Department that if they would assist me with the costs of completing the work, that I would let them have all the data I had gathered. I was told that my suggestion would be submitted to the committee.

I did not hear anything for a few weeks, and then on 29th May 1998 I received a letter from Pete King, the Principal Immigration Officer for the Falkland Islands Government, telling me that my residency application had been suspended because Falklands Conservation had accused me of data theft. I could hardly believe it, and immediately wrote to the Falkland Islands Government asking who had made the accusation, and what I was supposed to have stolen. They refused to tell me the name of the person who had made the accusation, or the nature of the accusation.

I made a few enquiries, and was told by the Chief Executive that the accusation had been made verbally at the Executive Council meeting by a member of Executive Council. Since Pete King had told me that the accusation had come from a member of Falklands Conservation, I immediately thought of Councillor Lewis Clifton. He was not only Chairman of Falklands

Conservation, and the person who had threatened to have me kicked out of the Falklands as an undesirable, but also a member of the Falkland Islands Government's Executive Council. I asked the Falkland Islands Government to confirm whether it was Councillor Clifton who had made the allegation, but they refused to tell me, saying that it was not in the public interest.

I then spoke to Magnus George, who was one of the trustees of Falklands Conservation. He told me that Lewis Clifton had been saying that the data I had offered to sell to the Environmental Planning Department had been stolen from Falklands Conservation. I assured Magnus that it had not, and asked him what Coastline Sensitivity Surveys Falklands Conservation had ever conducted. He did not know, so I told him to check with the office staff, since it was a fact that Falklands Conservation had never ever conducted ANY Coastline Sensitivity Surveys at ANY time in their history. It was therefore absolutely impossible for my data to have ever been the property of Falklands Conservation. The accusation of theft was not only nonsense, but appeared to be nothing more than a deliberate attempt to smear my reputation through rumour and false accusation.

I immediately wrote to Tom Eggeling, the Environmental Planning Officer, to ask how Falklands Conservation could have been sent details of my confidential funding application. He pointed out that Jeremy Smith sat on the committee that had considered my application, but added that such information should have been kept confidential. It was clear that Jeremy Smith had breached this confidentiality, and passed it on to the trustees of Falklands Conservation, who had decided that such a project posed a threat to their position as the Falklands' only government recognised conservation organisation.

I asked Tom Eggeling if Councillor Clifton, or any other member of Falklands Conservation, had written to him accusing me of stealing these data. He confirmed that just one day prior to the accusation being made to Executive Council, Councillor Clifton had written to him accusing me of stealing the Coastline Sensitivity Data that I had offered to provide. I asked him to confirm this in writing, which he did. He also confirmed that following receipt of this accusation from Clifton my application for funding had been rejected.

Now that I knew what the accusation comprised of, I was able to prove that it was not only untrue, but also a malicious fabrication made to discredit me, and to sabotage my attempts to gain residency and funding for my research. On 17th July I instructed my solicitor to prepare a case for libel and slander against Falklands Conservation, and on 13th August 1998 Falklands Conservation withdrew the allegation. They wrote to Executive Council and myself, apologising for any suggestion that I had committed theft, or otherwise behaved dishonestly. They stated that they had no outstanding grievances against me.

I told my solicitor that I still wished to sue Councillor Lewis Clifton for making the allegations. I had it in writing that my residency had been suspended on the sole basis of this accusation, and my funding application had also been turned down after a similar accusation had been made to the Environmental Planning Department. There was no way that

Councillor Clifton could justify accusing me of theft, and I felt that I was owed a personal apology at the very least. Unfortunately the local solicitors made it clear that they did not wish to pursue a slander case against a government official, such as Clifton, who had too many powerful friends.

On 31st August 1998, Pete King notified me that Executive Council had reconsidered my residency application, and had extended the period of suspension from 3 months to 2 years, despite the allegations being retracted. When I asked what the grounds were for suspending my application, he refused to tell me. It was quite clear to me that the reason for the suspension was that I was a thorn in their side over environmental protection. I was convinced that if they had had any justifiable grounds that would have stood up to scrutiny, they would have divulged them, just as they had done 3 months earlier over the Falklands Conservation allegation. By denying me the reason for their decision they were denying me the right to challenge the legitimacy of their decision, a clear breach of human rights under Falklands law.

My solicitor wrote to the Falkland Islands Government insisting that it was my right to know the reason for the suspension, so that I had a chance to defend myself. He pointing out that they had already refused to disclose the reason for refusing my application in 1997. The Attorney General had acknowledged that this had been a violation of human rights under International Law, and had instructed Executive Council that they could not refuse my application again without stating the reason. So instead of refusing my application they had suspended it, which they felt negated their obligation to give a reason. Despite my solicitors insistence, the Falkland Islands Government still refused to give a reason.

In September 1998 I returned from another fieldwork trip to Chile, and as soon as I got back home to the Falklands I immediately sensed that somebody had been in my room. At first it did not appear that anything had been taken, but upon closer inspection I discovered that 3 video tapes were missing. They were blue movies which I had brought with me from Britain, so I did not feel inclined to report the loss to the police. The videos did not contain anything that could not be bought or rented at shops in the Falklands, so I was not concerned about reporting the matter from a legal aspect. Even so, burglaries were uncommon in the Falklands, and it would have been a major news item. I did not want the local paper carrying headlines such as "Bingham loses pornographic videos in break-in", so I did not report the loss.

A week later I was writing up the results of my South American penguin census for a *Scientia Marina* article, and needed some old survey reports which I had stored under my bed. As I pulled out a few boxes to get to the reports, I noticed a small item wrapped up in cloth which I did not recognise. I unwrapped the cloth and found a 9mm pistol.

In novels I had often read the expression "his blood ran cold", but now I know what that feels like. That is exactly the sensation I felt as I sat staring at the pistol. A whole range of emotions and feelings swirled around in my head, with fear being the most forceful. It was obvious that the pistol had not been put under my bed as an early Christmas present. It had been put there for a reason, and that reason was obviously for it to be found, but not by me.

Nearby I found two cartons of bullets. My first reaction was panic, but I assured myself that they must have been there for at least a week, so I should slow down and act calmly. I carefully searched everywhere to see if anything else had been planted, but found nothing else.

Now I had to decide what to do with the gun. My first reaction was to dump it, but I was not sure whether or not that would be illegal. I considered taking it to the police station, but I was not sure whether or not they would believe my story. I knew from my residency application that the Falkland Islands Government wanted me out of their hair, and this would provide them with the ideal opportunity.

Despite the serious reservations that I had about disposing of vital evidence, I decided that the best course of action was to dump the pistol and ammunition at sea. Without wasting any further time I drove down to Gypsy Cove, and walked along to Engineer Point, where I threw them into the ocean.

The following day I made an appointment to see Governor Richard Ralph to express my concern that my dispute with Falklands Conservation and Falkland Islands Government was getting out of hand. A meeting was scheduled for 5th October 1998, and the Attorney General, David Lang, was also present.

I explained the events which had led to the dispute, and told the Governor and Attorney General that

I had reason to believe that a smear campaign had been launched against me by members of Falklands Conservation and government. I complained at the way in which false allegations had been used by Executive Council as grounds for suspending my residency permit, and said I believed the accusations to have been the result of personal and financial motives by Clifton. I complained that having cleared my name of the allegations which had led to the suspension, Executive Council had extended the suspension from 3 months to 2 years, and denied me the right to know the grounds for the decision. I then stated that I had reason to believe that my property was about to be searched in an attempt to frame and deport me.

The Governor stated that he had heard about my dispute with Councillor Clifton. He agreed that it was unfortunate that Councillor Clifton, after making threats against me, had been party to both the interview panel that had terminated my employment with Falklands Conservation, and the Executive Council which had suspended my residency application. He told me that he was unable to divulge the grounds for suspending my residency application, but he did acknowledge that it was now accepted that I was innocent of the accusations made by Clifton.

The Governor told me that he had already indicated to Executive Council that he was unhappy about the way that they had handled the matter, and suggested that if I resubmitted my application, he would instruct Executive Council to either make a decision, or to reveal the reasons for not doing so. He also assured me that he would not tolerate any use of police or government officials to hound an individual, and that if my prediction that my property was about to be searched turned out to be true, that he would investigate the matter most thoroughly.

I left the meeting feeling reassured. I felt that the Governor and Attorney General were both acting impartially, and that they would indeed step in if other agencies started to abuse their power in an attempt to frame me for some crime. I immediately did as the Governor had suggested, and submitted a second application to the Principal Immigration Officer, Pete King.

The following day I had a meeting with Magnus George, who was representing Falklands Conservation. We suggested a number of ways for co-operation, but I also discovered new allegations being made against me by Councillor Clifton. This got me thinking about the situation all over again, and I began to wonder if the Governor and Attorney General could possibly be involved. I decided that instead of putting all my faith in these men, I should take additional precautions to cover myself in case the Governor failed to keep his promise. I still believed that whoever planted the pistol was going to arrange for a search of my property, and if nothing was found, who knows what they might do next.

I wrote to the local newspaper office, Penguin News, stating that despite having never been arrested for anything in my entire life, I feared that my property was about to be searched in an attempt to frame me and deport me on false charges. Penguin News refused to print the story, so I went down to see them in person. I chatted to the Assistant Editor, Tony Burnett, and explained the history of what had happened. He was very sympathetic. I explained how Councillor Clifton had threatened to kick me out of the Falklands as an undesirable, and was then on the government committee that had refused my residency because of a false allegation which Clifton himself had made. Tony became more and more interested. He agreed to let me insert a letter asking for Clifton to explain his false allegations, and when Clifton declined to respond, Tony realised that something under-handed was going on within government and wrote a very damning editorial.

The Penguin News editorial of 13th November 1998 stated:

"Several weeks ago the Penguin News was presented with information alleging that a certain councillor had mounted an insidious campaign to deprive an individual of his job and the right to continue living in the Falkland Islands. Moreover the campaign was alleged to have included what are known in political circles as 'dirty tricks', which took the form of false accusations to third parties of dishonesty. It is a situation ripe to breed mistrust and suspicion, and one which will give birth to other more penetrating questions than simply asking if what is alleged is true or not, though that could be bad enough. Is this an isolated case of mis-use of power and position, or are there other cases? If the councillor is innocent of any wrong-doing, it is the least the councillor can do to restore his good name. And if the councillor has done

nothing that would bring discredit, then he has nothing to fear from making a full and frank disclosure."

Councillor Clifton refused to answer the allegations, but instead launched an attack against the paper's integrity, so the Penguin News editorial of 20th November 1998 went on to state:

"There was little doubt in the editorial mind that the Penguin News would receive a written response to last week's paper from at least one councillor, and so it proved. Sadly the response did not address the very important issues raised in the editorial, but took the form of an attack on the paper. Councillor Clifton signs his letter 'Disappointed'. Disappointed he may be, but not so much as those of the electorate who would have liked to have seen some sort of response from someone in authority to refute or explain the issues raised in last week's Penguin News."

I also wrote to several UK newspapers explaining the situation I was in, and predicting that the police were about to raid my home looking for planted evidence that I had already discovered and disposed of.

On 14th November I went to Chile again to do penguin counts on Isla Magdalena. I arrived back in the Falklands on 21st November, and within an hour of getting home the search which I had predicted occurred.

Customs Officers forced their way in with a search warrant, issued on the premise that a pornographic video had been discovered in my mail during a "routine mail check." It soon became clear that the video in question was one of the videos that had been stolen from my room during the break-in. Whoever had taken it had arranged to have it posted back to me from Britain, where Customs Officers just happened to be waiting for it.

The Customs Officers searched my property from top to bottom, but did not find the pistol or ammunition they were expecting. They did however confiscate an 18th century sword that had been in my family for 3 generations, on the basis that it was an offensive weapon! They were later forced to return the sword; presumably when somebody who understood the law told them to grow up.

The following day I flew out to Saunders Island at 8am to continue my penguin counts. I contacted Tony Burnett in the Penguin News office by phone as soon as I arrived, to let him know that my prediction had come true about the search. I sensed that he now knew what a serious case of corruption we were dealing with, and he told me that he was launching an investigation.

When I finally finished my research and returned to Stanley, I began to learn more about the way in which the authorities had gathered the excuse needed to search my property. On 3rd December I was called to the police station to be interviewed by the Customs Officers about the video they had found in the post. They showed me the video, and I was able to confirm that it was one of the videos that had been taken from my room in September.

Sometime after being taken from my room, it had been sent to Britain, where somebody had posted it back to me by Registered Mail. The Customs had coincidentally conducted a 'routine check' of parcels on the exact day the parcel had arrived, and opened it because it bore a registered mail sticker, but NO customs declaration sticker. The sender could not have advertised the parcel more clearly if he had written "CONTAINS ILLEGAL MATERIAL" in red ink.

It was not illegal to own the video, either in Britain or in the Falklands, but it was illegal to have such a video sent through the mail. By removing the video from my room and posting it back to me from an anonymous address, they had made an offence out of something that wasn't. What is more, the burden of proof seemed to lie with me proving that the video had been posted by a third party. This of course was impossible to prove without the help of the Governor or Attorney General.

I approached both the Governor and Attorney General to ask them to give evidence in court regarding the meeting we had held on 5th October 1998. The Governor was "too busy to see me", and the Attorney General, David Lang, told me *"I do remember us having a meeting Mr Bingham, but I don't recall the details of our conversation."*

I was furious. I knew that David Lang attended church regularly, and instructed my solicitor to call Lang as a hostile witness, so that he would be forced to stand up in court with his hand on the Bible and repeat his denial of our discussion. I also wanted to make him undergo a lie-detector test, but my solicitor told me I was living in Cuckoo Land. He gave me a huge ticking off for asking David Lang to give evidence, and told me to forget my conspiracy theories and to concentrate on the actual charge. That was all very well, but it left me with no defence.

CHAPTER FIFTEEN

On 20th January 1999, a Customs Officer served me with a warrant dated 12th January, for me to appear in court on charges of receiving prohibited items in the post. The day before the case was due to be heard in court I again phoned the Attorney General to ask him to give evidence regarding the conversation we had held at Government House. He refused, and later that evening I received an e-mail which stated

"Plead guilty tomorrow, and you might just survive this. - Friendly Advice"

I had already decided to plead guilty, since there was no way that I could prove the manner in which the video had been sent to me, with both the Governor and Attorney General refusing to give evidence. A long protracted court case discussing the global travels of my pornographic video was the last thing I needed. Better to accept a fine than be ridiculed in the press. The e-mail message merely served to convince me that I had made the right decision.

On 27th January 1999 I attended Stanley Magistrate's Court, and pleaded guilty to the charge of receiving a prohibited item through the post. The Senior Magistrate, Keith Watson, asked the Customs Officer giving evidence how it was that they had come to select my parcel for examination, and why I had not been given the opportunity to attend during the inspection. The Customs Officer replied that they had been alerted by the fact that the parcel had been sent by Registered Mail without the necessary Customs Declaration.

The Senior Magistrate said that he accepted that Customs Officers had acted within the framework of the law, but he added that it was in his opinion a very strange way of conducting an investigation. He stated that the video involved was not in itself illegal, and that it was not even obscene. He said that at most it could only be regarded as indecent, and even then only at the very lowest level of what could be described as indecent. He asked if the Crown Prosecution agreed with his assessment of the situation, and they acknowledged that they did. I was therefore fined £50 (US$75), the minimum fine permitted under the law for such an offence.

I was delighted with the outcome, and knew that I had made the right decision to plead guilty. It was clear that the Senior Magistrate was suspicious of the way the evidence had been gathered, and had stated so. He had also put on record that the video was not obscene, and could barely even be described as indecent. The Senior Magistrate's perception of the case against me had been indicated by the level of fine he had given; less than half that given to motorists caught speeding.

I knew full well that certain individuals within the Falkland Islands Government had gone to great lengths to bring serious charges against me, in order to have me deported. They had taken a serious risk by planting a firearm in my room, and had achieved nothing more than a negligible fine which could not possibly effect my residency. I hoped that after having taken such a risk and failed, that they would now let sleeping dogs lie. Unfortunately they were so convinced that their power placed them above the law, that they began resorting to increasingly bizarre ways of trying to deport me.

Just three days after the court hearing I received a phone call from an anonymous caller.

"I understand that you have some videos for sale." the caller said. It was the voice of a young male, in his late teens or early twenties. "I saw your advert in Penguin News..... From Amsterdam weren't they? You must be pretty pissed off to have lost them."

"Who's speaking please?" I enquired, thinking it was just a prankster.

"Nobody....." There was a pause. " I suppose you think this is the end of the matter do you?"

"I hope so yes." I replied

"Well it's not, its just the beginning...... We will keep after you until we get you out of our hair for good."

"Why are you doing this?" I asked, but the caller hung up.

There was little doubt that the call was from someone connected with the trouble, so I contacted the police to have them trace the call. Unfortunately the Falklands telephone system did not have any facility for tracing past calls. They did however offer to put a device on the phone that would trap the caller if he called again.

I agreed, and the police made the necessary arrangements. All I had to do was press a button when the caller was on the line, and the lines would be locked together until the caller was traced. The device was called an MCI, a Malicious Calls Interceptor. I did not really believe that the caller would try it again, but I was wrong.

Just three days later the caller did phone back.

"You're not getting the message are you? You're still causing trouble. Why don't you leave the Falklands now before you get thrown out?" It was the same voice as before, and I pressed the button. The phone lines locked, and I heard panic on the other end of the line as the caller realised something unexpected had happened.

Because I had locked my phone line to that of the caller, I had to go out to a public phone to notify the police that I had caught the caller. They told me that they would call me back with the results of the trace. Forty minutes later I was told that an error had been made during the trace, and that the identity of the caller had been "accidentally" lost.

I was furious, and very suspicious. Following the planting of the firearm, and the use of a stolen video tape to gain the search warrant to look for it, I knew that people within the justice system were involved, and I was not convinced that the caller's identity had been lost by "accident". I was convinced that the call had been traced back to someone who could not be identified for political reasons; somebody whose identity would be an embarrassment if put on trial for harassment.

A few days later I was arrested again. I was working on my house when two police officers called round, and told me I was being arrested for deception under the Thefts Act. I was taken down to Stanley Police Station, and told that I had been arrested for making a false statement about my qualifications on a job application form. I was taken into the interview room, and shown a copy of a job application form which the investigating officer, Jonathan Butler, said was mine.

The application form presented as evidence was sealed in plastic, with the section bearing my signature hidden from sight. The only section that was visible was the section listing qualifications, and it did indeed make a false statement about my qualifications, but I did not believe for a minute that it was my actual application form. I told the investigating officer that I believed the document to be falsified, and that I was not prepared to answer any more questions until I had a chance to check it out. I was eventually released and allowed to go home.

On 6th February 1999, I flew to Chile to get married to Elena. It should have been the happiest day of my life, but the wedding was marred by the thought that the Falklands police were now involved in a witch hunt to deport me from the Falklands, using any means at their disposal. I had now been able to confirm that the document presented by the police was indeed a forgery, and it was frightening to think that the Falklands Police would resort to such tactics.

Elena and I spent the first few days in Punta Arenas. On Monday 8th February we went to the Punta Arenas Registry Office, where we held the civil ceremony which made our marriage legal. Then we flew north to Concepcion, and on by bus to the tiny village of Los Alamos, where our actual wedding ceremony was to take place. This was Elena's home town, and we stayed with her parents until the wedding.

Los Alamos is a very rural area, and it was like stepping back in time. Very few of the houses had telephones, and horses and carts were still being used to transport goods. Elena had lived near to Los Alamos throughout her childhood.

A couple of days before our wedding Elena took me to a nearby forestry plantation, and explained that it was the site where she had grown up as a child. It had once been a lively town called Pilpilco, with its own hospital, schools, police station, and all the things that make up town life. Most of the population had been employed by the mining industry, and Elena's father had also been a miner. When the mines closed down the land was sold for forestry, and the people were evicted from their homes. The whole town had been reduced to rubble by machinery, and a forestry plantation planted in its place.

It was an eerie feeling to walk along forestry tracks, as Elena pointed out where the school had once been, and where her house had stood. At the site of her house we found remnants of roof tiles, an old kitchen stove and various household artefacts. I was choked to see how a whole community had been destroyed in such a callous way to make room for forestry plantations. I can barely imagine how Elena must have felt looking through the remains of what had once been her home.

Following the mass eviction, Elena and her family had moved to the neighbouring village of Los Alamos, where they had remained. Their house was fairly large, which was just as well since Elena had eleven brothers and sisters, several of whom had come to Los Alamos for the wedding. Unfortunately nobody had made the actual arrangements for the wedding, despite assuring Elena that they had. It was two days prior to the wedding, and there was no wedding cake or photographer, and even the church had not been booked.

The vicar told us that the Sunday we had requested was not possible since he had a service in another district. We did not wish to change the date, because our wedding had been planned for Valentine's Day. Elena's family had assured us that the church and vicar had been booked. Now they were saying it didn't matter if we had the wedding on Saturday instead. I assured them that it did. Eventually we managed to find another vicar who was able to hold the ceremony on the Sunday, and we managed to get our wedding cake and photographer arranged with hours to spare.

On the morning of the wedding Elena went to her brother's house to prepare, and I went to Lebu to book the hotel for our honeymoon. I also placed a wedding present, a bottle of champagne, and a large bouquet of flowers on the bed, ready for our arrival after the wedding. I did not get back to Elena's parents' house until 30 minutes before the wedding, and they were all panicking that I was going to be late. They should have worried more about their own arrangements than mine. Fifteen minutes later I was in my suit and all ready to go. My chauffeur however, was not.

At 7pm, the time when I should have been in church, Elena's brother who was driving me to the church was still not ready. I did not arrive at the church until 7.20pm, 20 minutes late. I needn't have worried however, because Elena was 40 minutes late. Nobody seemed to care - this was Chile.

Elena looked absolutely stunning in her cream lace wedding dress, escorted by her elder brother. The service was conducted in Spanish in traditional Chilean style. After the wedding our chauffeur drove us up and down the village in the car, which by now had been decorated with ribbons, streamers, tin cans and lots of writing. Everybody in the village waved and cheered as we were driven along the high street and around the back streets.

Eventually we arrived at Elena's brother's house, where the reception had been laid on. It was a large house, but the sheer number of people filled it to capacity. Finally at 1.30am, after much drinking, eating and dancing, we were driven to our hotel in nearby Lebu. Elena was shocked to find a large bunch of flowers, a present and a bottle of champagne waiting on the bed, as I carried her over the threshold into our hotel room.

We opened the champagne, and Elena opened her present; a very pretty negligee. Despite the problems lurking back home for me, I had at least been able to put them out of my mind for this special occasion. Our honeymoon passed all too rapidly, and the following weekend I returned to the Falklands, with Elena and her nine year old son, to begin married life.

As soon as I got back to the Falklands, I had the feeling that somebody had been through my house again. I conducted a thorough search to see if anything else had been planted, but could find nothing. I just felt in my bones that the police and the government were plotting something else, but I couldn't figure out what.

I decided that what I needed was outside help, someone who would sniff out scandal and corruption if something else happened. I therefore wrote to a number of UK newspapers, explaining how I had been asked to fabricate data to cover up penguin declines, and how I had been threatened with losing my job and deportation from the Falklands if I refused. I told them how I had lost my job a few weeks later, and how since then I had been set up on false charges of importing an indecent video, and narrowly avoided being framed on charges of possession of a firearm and making a false statement on an application form.

I said in my letters that I did not expect the reporters to take my story seriously at this stage, but asked them to keep my letter on file and await developments. I explained that if I was correct, something else would happen shortly, and they would then know they had a worthy story. I told them that despite having never been in trouble with the police in all my life prior to coming to the Falklands, that I strongly suspected I was going to be framed again very soon.

Two days later I was woken at 4.40am by a phone call. I fully expected it to be another malicious call, but it wasn't. It was my father, giving me the dreadful news that my sister's husband had been killed. My father was in tears as he told me how Martin had been on his way to work in the morning, when his Landrover had skidded into the back of a lorry stopped at traffic lights on the brow of a hill. He had died at the scene; how quickly was uncertain.

I was absolutely numb from the news. I found it hard to feel grief initially. It was as though the connection between the part of my mind that knew it to be true, had failed to transmit the message to the part of my brain which responded emotionally. It was only the following morning that I began to feel the deep sense of loss.

Martin had been a very close and well loved member of the family, ever since he had married Alison. They had had the perfect marriage. They had done everything together, pursuing the same careers as archaeologists, and always being fortunate enough to find work together. They had barely been apart in nearly 20 years. I knew that Alison would be devastated, and felt so utterly useless being so far away.

I found it hard to concentrate on my work for many days, and this state would have continued for some time if the Falkland Islands Government had not committed another travesty of justice, turning my sorrow into anger.

On 3rd March 1999 I was doing the afternoon shift in the power station when one of the Customs Officers, Jenny Smith, called at work to see me. She had previously asked my boss for permission to arrest me there in front of my work colleagues, in preference to doing it in the privacy of my home. As soon as she arrived at my work place she cautioned me, and told me that I was being charged with another incident of deception. I thought it must be related to the document which the police had arrested me for a few weeks previously, but it was not.

She gave me a number of documents which I had submitted to the Customs & Immigration Department over the years relating to my residency applications.

She asked me to look through the documents carefully, and tell her if the statements made were all true. I felt a chill go down my spine, wondering if perhaps somewhere I had made an error, or a statement that differed between applications. I studied the documents carefully, but could find no discrepancies or errors.

Jenny Smith pointed out that I had stated no previous criminal convictions on all of the forms. I agreed, wondering what they could have found wrong with that. Jenny then told me that they had received information that I had previous criminal convictions for burglary, car theft and affray. I burst out laughing, largely from utter relief that it was another act of incompetence on their behalf, rather than anything serious.

Jenny Smith did not find the matter so amusing, and handed me a list of criminal convictions, giving dates and court convictions, with my name at the top. I told her that I had never been convicted of any of the offences, and suggested that it should not be difficult to prove. A phone call to the relevant court was all that was required to confirm the convictions were not mine. Perhaps realising that something was not right, she told me that I would not be placed under arrest in my work place, but that I should present myself at the police station at the end of my shift for fingerprinting. The fingerprints would be sent to Interpol to prove whether or not the convictions were mine.

I went to the police station as instructed, and my fingerprints were taken. I also sent my father an e-mail telling him what had happened. I gave him the list of convictions which Jenny Smith had given me, and asked him to contact his local police for assistance. I did not trust the Falklands police at all after everything that had happened. It was clear that they were part of a witch hunt to deport me, and were not too fussy about the methods being used. The following day my father faxed me through a request form, which I had to sign in order for the British police to conduct the search.

A couple of days later I went to the Post Office to collect my mail, and received a very frosty reception from people I met. People I normally chatted to cut me off cold, and people I didn't know were staring at me. As I came out of the Post Office, I nearly bumped into an elderly lady who I didn't even recognise. She stepped back and spat at me.

"We don't need your kind here." She said as she pushed past me. "Go back to where you came from".

It had now become public belief that I was a convicted burglar, but how? I was angry that Jenny Smith had asked my boss for permission to arrest me at work, rather than tackle me about the matter at home, and I thought she must have discussed the matter with my work colleagues when she had come to arrest me, but I soon found out the truth.

Apparently soon after she had come to my work place to caution me and interview me, she had gone and discussed the matter in the public bar of the Stanley Arms. It is difficult to see why a long-serving Customs Officer would go to a public bar and notify the public that I was a convicted burglar, unless the intention was to stir up hatred towards me. Since the allegation was untrue, the Falkland Islands Government would never have been able to use it as grounds to deport me, so it seemed likely that the public hatred stirred up by these false allegations was the real aim. This hatred was also targeted towards my wife and 9 year old step-son, who had just arrived from Chile to begin their new life in the Falklands.

On 11th March I was called to attend yet another interview at Stanley Police Station with my solicitor. It was a complete waste of time because the Customs and Immigration Officer handling the case failed to show. I did however discover where the Customs & Immigration Department had got the information about my convictions. It had come from the Falkland Islands Police. What a surprise!

Apparently the Falkland Islands Police, having previously done a "routine check" on my mail, and a "routine check" on all my old application forms, had decided to do a "routine check" to see if I had any previous convictions or other skeletons in my closet. Of course the fact that the Falklands Police were looking through every document I had ever signed, and every action I had ever taken, in search of reasons to arrest me, was all entirely routine. The police insisted that it was in no way connected to the threat made by Councillor Clifton to kick me out of the Falklands as an undesirable if I did not keep quiet about the decline in penguins.

Jock Elliott, of the Falkland Islands Police, claimed that Interpol had faxed him a list of convictions against my name, but I did not believe him, so I demanded the name of the person in Interpol who had sent him the list. He was reluctant to give me the name, and told me that if I had no such convictions that I had nothing to worry about. I told him that since the public had now been told by one of the Customs and Immigration Officers that I was a convicted burglar, that I had every reason to worry, and would be doing my own investigation. I again demanded the name and address of the person in Interpol who had sent him the list of convictions, and Elliott was finally forced to give me it. I immediately wrote to Interpol asking if they had told the Falklands Police I was a convicted burglar, and if so why.

A few days later my father sent through the results of the investigation by the British Police. They confirmed that I had no criminal convictions whatsoever. My father also faxed down the court records for the convictions listed on the sheet which Jenny Smith had given me. It showed clearly that the convictions belonged to a totally different person. The person did have the surname Bingham, but a Bingham that was 2 years older with different first names.

I was now very suspicious about the validity of the whole investigation. Any search of criminal records would invariably use date of birth, otherwise people such as Jenny Smith would have thousands of convictions to her name. I did not believe that another error could have occurred by accident, so soon after framing me over the video, the attempt to frame me with the firearm, and the use of a false application form.

I went down to the Police Station and showed Jock Elliott the documents from the British Police and the Courts. He told me that he had still had no reply regarding my fingerprints, so he could not be certain of my innocence. I urged him to get his finger out, since my family and I were suffering a lot of public abuse from people who had been led to believe that I was a convicted criminal. I told him that I would be expecting a public apology when they finally confirmed their "mistake".

Elena's son, Juan, started at his new school on 31st March 1999, and the teachers were absolutely wonderful with him. He made an excellent start, helped by the fact that he had learned quite a lot of English before he came to the Falklands. The only problem Juan faced was hassle from other children who thought I was a criminal.

Children can be very cruel, and tend to pick up on whatever parents are saying about people at home. Juan got constantly teased and harassed with comments such as "your dad's a burglar", "we don't need your sort here" and "go back to where you came from". Needless to say he found it very upsetting, and Elena urged me to sort out the problem as soon as possible. Elena also started getting phone calls from so called "friends" telling her to be careful of me.

Coming out of West Store a few days later, I heard a couple of people chatting together, and immediately recognised one of the voices as the person who had made the malicious calls. It was one of the Customs & Immigration Officers, and I immediately contacted the Director of Customs & Immigration and told him that I had identified Russell as the malicious caller. I made an official complaint and was told that the matter would be investigated. I also checked the legal position, and confirmed that voice recognition was just as admissible in court as eye witness recognition.

I then went to Stanley Police Station to again demand that they acknowledge that the convictions did not belong to me, so that my family and I could begin our married life in peace. I pointed out that my wife and her 9 year old son were being harassed as a direct result of their incompetence, if not corruption, but they were completely unmoved. I was told that they had still not received a reply from Interpol, and that they could take no action until they did. I made it clear that I thought they were deliberately stalling, and using the harassment of my wife and stepson as a tactic to force me to leave.

Finally on 15th April, Jock Elliott phoned me up to say that Interpol had confirmed that the convictions had belonged to a totally different person, just as I had stated all along. I told him that I wanted it in writing, and that I wanted an official apology. He told me that he was unable to put it in writing, since Interpol had confirmed my innocence by phone. I pointed out that unless it was put in writing and made public, that people would continue to believe I was a criminal, and continue to harass my family. I reminded him that a 9 year old boy was being harassed as a result of their actions, but he told me it was not his problem.

He told me to take the matter up with the Customs Officer who had been responsible for letting the public know. Needless to say the Customs & Immigration Department blamed the Falkland Islands Police for sending them false information, saying that they had acted in good faith on the information the Falkland Islands Police had provided. The Falkland Islands Police blamed the Customs & Immigration Department, and the Customs & Immigration Department blamed the Falkland Islands Police. Neither were prepared to take responsibility for notifying the public that I was not a convicted burglar, and my wife and child continued to suffer harassment.

Exactly seven days later, a Police Officer came to my house and served me with a warrant to appear in court charged with the previous offence of making a false statement on a job application form. I had assumed that after proving that the application form presented as evidence at my interview was fabricated, that the charges had been dropped, but that was not the case. They were now trying to revitalise the case by getting Falklands Conservation to say that I had lied about my qualifications on their application form. Needless to say, after all that had happened, Falklands Conservation were only too willing to oblige.

Falklands Conservation agreed to provide three witnesses, Dr John Croxall, Julian Fitter and Carol (Hay) Miller, who were willing to perjure themselves by saying that I had lied about my qualifications during my interview 6 years previously. They presumably thought it would be my word against theirs, with them having the upper hand with regard to numbers. Fortunately I had something which they did not have - concrete evidence.

Falklands Conservation's accusation was that during my interview in June 1993 I had claimed to have completed my Open University degree, when in fact I did not complete my final exams until November 1993. They clearly assumed that what took place during an interview 6 years before would have been my word against theirs, but they had forgotten one vital fact. Falklands Conservation had actually arranged transport for me to take my final exams at the Military Education Centre, 2 weeks after I had begun my employment with them in October 1993. Carol (Hay) Miller, the Secretary of Falklands Conservation, had even written a letter to me in September 1993 (one month before I began my employment) confirming that transport to my Open University exams would be provided by Falklands Conservation after commencement of my employment.

Mrs Miller, along with Croxall and Fitter, must have forgotten about the existence of this letter, because she gave the Falkland Islands Police a sworn statement stating that she had no knowledge of me taking any exams, and that I had misled her into thinking I had finished my degree course. Shortly after Croxall, Fitter and Miller gave their sworn statements to the Falkland Islands Police, the Falklands Police came across Miller's letter amongst Falklands Conservation's files, proving that Falklands Conservation had been fully aware that I had not completed my degree course at the time of my appointment.

Clearly Croxall, Fitter and Miller could no longer go to court and state under oath that I had claimed to hold a degree during my interview, when a letter written by themselves three months later acknowledged that they knew full well that I had not completed my degree at the time of my employment. The case against me effectively collapsed, except for one minor detail. Instead of making the discovery of this letter known to me or my solicitor, the Falkland Islands Police denied its existence, and even stated in writing that no such letter had been found. They kept it hidden in their case file for 4 years, until a Supreme Court hearing into government corruption in October 2003 finally forced them to hand it over.

Prior to discovering that their case had gone pear-shaped, the crown prosecution announced to the press that I had been charged with deception under the Theft Act. Once again I suffered ridicule, and more important, Juan and Elena were subjected to increased levels of harassment. Any chance of a public apology from the police for the false accusations that I was a burglar had been put on hold until the court hearing, which was still several weeks away. A long time for Juan and Elena to hang on. My only comfort was that I knew I would have my day in court, and that people within Falklands Conservation and the Falkland Islands Government would be forced to commit perjury, which carries a mandatory prison sentence.

Having made the charges public, the Crown Prosecution then discovered the existence of the letter which proved my innocence. The Falkland Islands Police had now made three separate charges against me using false documentation and false testimony. They had arrested me on the basis of a document which the Falkland Islands Police had printed up themselves on the Police Station computer. Then they had arrested me and told the public that I was a convicted burglar, based on false information from the Falkland Islands Police. Now they had charged me with deception on the basis of false testimony given by prominent members of Falklands Conservation. Any legitimate investigation would see this as government and police corruption if the truth got out.

My father was terrified for my safety. He kept urging me to flee from the Falklands, pointing out that it was not unheard of for people with evidence of high-level corruption to be killed. I thought it unlikely, but I shared his concern that the authorities would resort to increasingly dishonest tactics to avoid prosecution for what they had done. I therefore wrote to Amnesty International, detailing the entire story from start to finish, and expressing my fears. They said that they were unable to take on the case themselves, because they only dealt with cases of physical violence and murder, but they did put me in touch with a more specialist organisation called Index on Censorship.

On 7th June 1999 I received a letter from the Attorney General, stating that the case against me was being withdrawn because it was not in the public interest to spend public money proceeding with the case at a time when government were experiencing financial difficulties. He was saying that I was to be presumed guilty, but that government could not afford to prosecute me in court because of financial hardship! I was absolutely furious. I immediately contacted my solicitor to see if there was any way that I could insist that the court case proceeded. He told me that there was not.

It was obvious that the decision to stop the court case had nothing to do with financial considerations. Shortly before David Lang's decision to withdraw the case on financial grounds, he had warned me in writing that if I lost the case I would have to pay all the government's expenses. This included the costs of bringing John Croxall and Julian Fitter from the UK, incurring costs of flights, hotels and lost earnings. Had I lost the case I would have been bankrupt, but I knew I would not loose. If Lang really did withdraw the charges for financial reasons, it could only have been because he knew he would loose the case, since that is the only way government would have been forced to bear the costs.

By now I was able to prove that the first job application form for which I had been arrested had been printed up on the Stanley Police Station computer. This false document had been used in place of the original, which had contained no dishonest statement. I could also prove that the authorities had used convictions belonging to a totally different person in an attempt to deport me from the Falklands. Finally I could show that Carol Miller, John Croxall and Julian Fitter of Falklands Conservation, had all given sworn statements to the police claiming that I had misled them into thinking I had completed my degree course, when Carol Miller herself had written to me offering transportation for me to sit my exams after the commencement of my employment. Had the court case gone ahead, these witnesses and police officers would have been forced to admit their mistakes, or commit perjury, which carried an automatic sentence of two years imprisonment. Perhaps the legal expenses of prosecuting these people for perjury was the financial consideration to which Attorney General David Lang had referred.

Just two days after the case against me was withdrawn, I received a letter from Interpol confirming in writing that the criminal convictions had belonged to a different person. The letter also stated that Interpol had informed the Falkland Islands Police from the very outset that these convictions belonged to a different person with a different date of birth. They had in fact notified the Falklands Police of this fact BEFORE Jenny Smith had even come to arrest me.

In a letter dated 30th July 1999, the Head of Interpol UK, David Wolstenholme wrote "*I am satisfied that in a telephone conversation on 8th January my office did tell the Falkland Islands Police that the identification we had found was not an exact match, and pointed out to them that we had a different date of birth.*"

I was furious and really fired up. I now had proof that the Falkland Islands Police had told the Customs Department that I had criminal convictions for burglary and other offences, when they had already been told by Interpol that I did not. I was determined to have the officers involved prosecuted. I went to see the Chief of Police, David Morris, and demanded copies of the tape recordings of my police interviews, which documented their false accusations and claims. I also demanded a copy of the false application form which had been presented as evidence during my interrogation.

I was now given the documents without question, and the Chief of Police, David Morris, finally admitted that my original application form had been swapped for a different one prior to my arrest. He said that ex-Chief of Police, Ken Greenland, had entered the details from my original application form onto the computer. By accident the details relating to my qualifications had been entered incorrectly, making it look as though I had lied about my qualifications. My original application form had then been mislaid by the police, so they had printed out a copy from their computer, passed it off as the original, and arrested me on the basis of the changes which they themselves had made, unaware that their "copy" was different from the original.

This was all just an administrative error. It was all shear coincidence that this had occurred at the exact same time that they were accusing me of having convictions that belonged to another person, charging me with deception on the basis of false statements from Falklands Conservation, and denying the existence of evidence in their own case file that proved my innocence.

I did not believe such a ridiculous explanation for one minute, and demanded an independent investigation to determine if this collection of incidents amounted to incompetence or corruption. The Chief of Police refused to conduct such an investigation. I therefore wrote to the Police Complaints Authority, outlining the whole series of events, and enclosing copies of the documentary evidence. I also made similar complaints to the Governor, the Customs & Immigration Department, the UK newspapers, the MP from my home constituency, and Index on Censorship. I also asked the Director of Customs & Immigration why I had heard nothing about my complaint against his officer, for making the malicious phone calls.

Two days after sending these letters, I crashed my Landrover on the Airport Road, because somebody had removed the wheel nuts from my front wheel whilst it was parked outside Stanley Airport. Fortunately I had not built up much speed at the time, and felt the wheel wobbling before it came off, so the accident was not serious. Four days later my car was sabotaged outside my work, when somebody cut through the clutch cable. Two weeks later somebody ripped out the dashboard wiring, and two weeks after that the engine block was filled to the brim with petrol through the oil filler cap.

Fortunately the excess petrol had leaked out of the dip stick holder causing a huge puddle of petrol under the car which alerted me to the problem prior to starting the engine. Had I started the engine without noticing, the petrol would have been blown all over the engine and been ignited by the ignition system, causing a fire ball. This not only threatened myself, but also my wife and her 9 year old son who also travelled in the car. This act demonstrated the kind of people I was dealing with.

Despite these obvious warnings, I was determined to press ahead with my quest for justice. I was outraged by the way that members of government and the justice system had committed acts of corruption, forgery and perjury in an attempt to pursue their personal and political agendas. I wanted the people responsible exposed, disgraced, sacked and prosecuted.

I also felt that a big story was the only way of showing the public that I had been innocent of the charges and rumours which had been brought against me over the past few months. The local newspaper and radio station had run a small announcement stating that my fingerprints were being destroyed, and that the police had mistaken somebody else's criminal convictions for mine. But there was no apology from the police, and by now the mixture of charges, accusations and rumours left the average man in the street totally confused. Most people assumed that after having been arrested so many times, I must have been guilty of something, even if the saga had become so complicated that it was hard to figure out what I was supposed to be guilty of.

In a large country that wouldn't have mattered so much, but in a tiny population it did. This was reflected by the harassment which my wife and stepson were still receiving. Juan in particular was finding it increasingly difficult to cope with the harassment.

Needless to say my calls for an investigation fell on deaf ears. The Governor and the Director of Customs & Immigration ignored my correspondence, even when I sent my complaints by registered post. The Police Complaints Authority wrote and told me that the Falkland Islands Police did not come under British jurisdiction. They told me that the Falkland Islands Police were not answerable to anybody except the Chief of Police and the Governor, neither of whom were willing to act for fear of self-incrimination.

Fortunately Index on Censorship and Dafydd Wigley MP were more interested. Index on Censorship concluded their investigation, and wrote a lengthy article in their September journal, whilst Dafydd Wigley MP raised the matter with the British Foreign Secretary, Robin Cook.

Although the Index on Censorship journal had a fairly limited distribution, many of its subscribers were news reporters looking for stories, so it was not long before the major British newspapers became interested in the story. The Guardian, Observer, Sunday Times and Daily Post all mounted an investigation, and it was just a matter of time before the whole sordid affair hit the British headlines.

I was pleased that the corruption and persecution which I had suffered following my refusal to cover up penguin declines was going to be exposed, but I was also worried about the backlash. It was one thing to protest locally, but quite another to have the Falkland Islands Government and Falkland Islands Police Force plastered across the British newspapers accused of corruption. I feared that I would suffer serious backlash, possibly even from members of the public who objected to having the reputation of the Falklands dragged through the mud.

By now Juan could no longer cope with the harassment, and wanted to go back to Chile. I had persuaded him for weeks to give it a bit longer, but with the prospect of things getting worse I could no longer do so with a clear conscience. Elena and I agreed to let him go back to Chile until things blew over, and on 9th October 1999 I accompanied Juan to Los Alamos in Chile, and left him with his grandparents. The Falkland Islands Government and Falkland Islands Police had succeeded in hounding a 9 year old child out of the Falklands.

Unknown to me, the numerous accusations made against me by the police since my wife's arrival in the Falklands had also taken their toll on our marriage. Believing that the police would not make up such accusations, Elena had begun having an affair with another man, whom she believed would make a better husband and father to her child than the 'criminal' she had married.

The British press really went to town with headlines such as "*Arrested, framed, accused and threatened - Researcher fights a one-man war in the Falklands*". The story first appeared in The Sunday Times and The Observer on Sunday 10th October 1999. This was followed by two articles in The Guardian, and articles in The Daily Post, The Mail on Sunday, Private Eye and Birdwatch magazine.

The articles varied in length from whole page features to single columns, exposing the Falklands authorities' corruption and persecution in great detail. In particular they told how I had been asked to falsify research data to cover up penguin declines, how I had been threatened with dismissal and how I had finally been dismissed as Conservation Officer on the grounds that I had "drawn too much attention to oiled birds". They told about the planting of firearms in my room to frame me, the fabrication of documentary evidence in the police station, the use of convictions belonging to another person in an attempt to deport me, and the refusal of the Governor and local justice departments to conduct an investigation.

The news reports pulled no punches, and spared nobody. The Falkland Islands Government, Falklands Conservation and the Falkland Islands Police were all humiliated, and exposed for the dirty deeds they had used against me. With so much bad publicity, the British Foreign & Commonwealth Office were left with no option but to act.

What was astonishing however, was the lack of response by the local Falklands newspaper, Penguin News. It usually reported any British newspaper article that made reference to the Falklands, and yet on this occasion, with the Falklands authorities, justice system and conservation organisation all being exposed as co-conspirators in wide-scale corruption, there was absolutely no mention of it whatsoever. This major event was never reported at all in the local newspaper. For the Falklands newspaper office it was as though the event had never happened.

However the Falklands newspaper office was government funded, and viewed in that light it was perhaps no surprise that the story was hushed up, just as Falklands Conservation, the government funded conservation organisation, had hushed up news of starving penguins, oil spills and over-fishing. It didn't really make much difference though, because so many Falklands people read British newspapers that such a major story could not be kept quiet. Surprisingly though, the hostility I had anticipated never materialised. On the contrary, most people were appalled by what had been done to me, and were very supportive of my plight.

Within a week of the story hitting the headlines, the British government sent a Police & Criminal Justice Advisor to the Falklands to conduct an inspection of the Falkland Islands Police. The Governor also wrote to me, apologising for having ignored my previous correspondence and asking to see me in order to sort out the matter.

The Police & Criminal Justice Advisor arrived in the Falklands on the afternoon of 19th October 1999, and at 8am the following morning the Falklands Chief of Police called me by phone to officially apologise for what had been done to me; no doubt with the British government's Police & Criminal Justice Advisor standing over him. He accepted that his officers had made a number of mistakes, but continued to insist that they had been administrative errors, rather than any deliberate attempt to frame me. He did agree however to make a written apology.

The Police & Criminal Justice Advisor completed his inspection and made a report itemising a number of ways to prevent a similar incident happening again. This report

1) stated that there was a need to strengthen police accountability through democratic process.
2) highlighted the lack of civilian oversight of the complaints procedure.
3) stated that complaints against the police needed to be independent, and must be seen by the public to be open and transparent.
4) recommended that the Governor establish a body to oversee the investigation of complaints made against the police.
5) pointed out that it was not good practice for the police to also act as prosecutors, and suggested the roles be undertaken independently.

Unfortunately none of these recommendations were ever adopted by the Falkland Islands Government or Police. However the Conservation Officer for Falklands Conservation, Jeremy Smith, resigned and left the Falklands. On 27th October 1999 the matter was raised in the Houses of Parliament, and John Battle

MP made a statement on behalf of the Falkland Islands Government. He stated that

"Mr Bingham has every right to complain that incorrect information concerning previous criminal convictions was used by the Falkland Islands Police. This was clearly an error. I regret any embarrassment caused to Mr Bingham." He added that "Falklands Conservation have unconditionally withdrawn any accusation they might have made."

CHAPTER SIXTEEN

Paramount Studios in Hollywood heard about the story through the British newspapers, and phoned me up asking if they could do a documentary about my work. I agreed, and their film crew arrived in the Falklands on 6th November 1999. The following day we flew out to Saunders Island which was one of my regular sites for conducting research work on penguins and albatross.

The programme was a fly-on-the-wall documentary series about wildlife conservationists, and the idea was for the camera to follow me around the island throughout the day, filming whatever I was doing. The camera was on me more than the wildlife, and I was asked to give a running commentary as I worked.

The day began by filming me filling up my thermos flask, a sequence which they wanted to shoot from outside the house through the kitchen window. It was a good job I wasn't actually putting any coffee in the flask during the shoot, because we had to shoot the sequence seven times.

The next shot they wanted to film was me walking out of the house with my rucksack. The cameraman wanted to film it from in front of me, which meant him walking backwards whilst filming. There were several turns between the kitchen and the front door, and on two occasions the cameraman fell over trying to back out. After six attempts and nearly thirty minutes, they finally got the 5 second clip they wanted, and we got underway. So much for "film it as it happens"!

The cross-country journey from the settlement to the seabird colony was the next bit to be filmed. Normally I did the work alone and used a motorcycle, but with the film crew in tow I had to use a 4x4 vehicle. The landowner's 13 year old daughter, Louise Pole-Evans, drove us out in their Landrover. About halfway to the seabird colony the film director stopped us to get a shot of the vehicle going along the track. Of course he selected the most rugged bit of the journey in which to get that special shot; a section where it was impossible to turn the vehicle around between re-takes. Every re-take meant reversing back over 500 metres of boulders and muddy hollows.

The film director, Rick Ringback, asked if I could drive the vehicle over this section rather than Louise, because it would look better for the programme if I was driving. That was no problem. I had often driven the Landrover along this track. I felt very embarrassed however when Rick asked Louise if she would crouch down beneath the dashboard so as not to be seen.

Fortunately Louise took it in good spirit, and the day's filming at the colony went well.

The following day the landowner, David Pole-Evans, took us to the penguin colonies at The Neck in an inflatable dinghy. On the way out Rick asked David to drop the cameraman on the shore, so that he could get a shot of us shooting past in the dinghy. As usual one shot was not enough, and we were subjected to the now familiar line of "Well that was great, but perhaps we could try it just one more time."

Having finally got to the site, David took the dinghy as close as he could up the sandy beach, but this still left us a few metres away from dry land, so David carried us on his back one by one from the dinghy to the shore. He then returned home to press on with running the farm, and we spent the day amongst the penguin colonies filming my work. David came back to collect us at 7.30pm, and once again he carried us one by one back from the shore to the dinghy. He started up the motor, and we set off home.

"Oh, I've forgotten the films" Announced the cameraman halfway home. When asked where he had left them, he pointed to the top of the mountain we had just climbed down. After much discussion it was agreed that we had no option but to go back, and David carried the cameraman from the dinghy back to the shore for the third time. David was then left standing in the surf up to his waist, holding the dinghy, whilst the cameraman ran back up the mountain to retrieve his films. Finally he returned with the films, and David carried him back into the dinghy for the fourth time. David's patience was beyond reproach. He never moaned at the cameraman once about the delay, which is more than could be said for the rest of us.

We spent three days filming my research on penguins, and the fourth day was spent on my albatross studies. Part of this work included putting identification rings on adult birds to monitor adult mortality, but the Falkland Islands Government had prevented me from continuing with this work by introducing a new law.

Bird ringing is a skilled job, and should only be conducted by somebody who is trained and experienced. I had held a ringing license from the British Trust of Ornithology for years, and this had permitted me to ring birds in the Falkland Islands since 1993. I was in fact the only person living in the Falklands to hold such a license.

In 1999 the Falkland Islands Government decided to change the law, and drafted new legislation which gave them responsibility for the issuing of bird ringing licenses. The new legislation they drafted affected just one person, myself. As a result, from 1st November 1999 I needed a license from the Environmental Planning Officer in order to continue my work, and I applied for my license the moment the new law was announced. I was told that despite it now being illegal for me to continue my work without the new license, that the Environmental Planning Officer was not yet ready to begin issuing licenses.

I made it clear that I needed the license by the beginning of November, in order for an assistant to fly across from Chile to help me with the work. I could not afford to pay the substantial costs of bringing an assistant from Chile unless I knew the work could proceed. Whether by incompetence or another deliberately attempt to stop my work, the license was not issued by the time my assistant was due to leave, and the research programme had to be cancelled. Then when the Environmental Planning Officer heard that I was being filmed for a documentary on cable TV, he phoned me to give me the permission I needed, presumably to prevent me complaining about more government harassment. Of course by now it was impossible for my assistant to join me.

This was in fact the second year that this project had been sabotaged. The previous year Dr John Croxall of Falklands Conservation had written to the project co-ordinators accusing me of various sins. Fauna & Flora International had withdrawn my funding as a result, and by the time I had proven that Dr Croxall's allegations were false and malicious, and had my funding re-instated, I had missed the deadline for the work.

In March 2000, the Falkland Islands Government finally admitted that they did not want to give me a licence to ring birds on Saunders Island because "it overlapped with work being done by Falklands Conservation", their government funded conservation organisation. In most countries independent research is encouraged by the government. When it is not, it usually means that they have something they want to hide.

One of the things which Paramount Pictures had come to film was the work on albatross, so since I now had permission to continue, but lacked an assistant, the Film Director, Rick Ringback, suggested that he could act as my assistant. Albatross are very easy to ring because they are large robust birds, and have absolutely no fear of people. One reason for this lack of fear is their huge hooked beak, which takes out chunks of skin each time it makes a strike. The moment you approach an albatross sitting on its nest it begins to snap its beak as a warning, and this behaviour can be used to catch the bird if you have the knack.

I showed Rick how to catch the beak in one hand, and take the bird over the back and wings with the other arm. With the beak and wings held closed, the bird was immobilised, with the legs pointing outwards ready for ringing. Easier said than done. Each time Rick got near the bird, he hesitated just a little too long, and the bird got him first. As the cameraman continued filming, Rick's injury count steadily mounted. Finally I called a halt to proceedings, whilst Rick still had some skin left on his arms. The albatross seemed most disappointed. It was just beginning to enjoy itself.

With the filming on Saunders Island now completed, we moved on to Volunteer Point, where the main population of King penguins was located. By early November the ten month old chicks appear larger than the adults and are covered in thick downy plumage. They look like giant teddy bears, and are a great attraction to tourists and wildlife photographers alike.

Not only do the chicks look comical, but they are also very curious of people. Almost as soon as one sits down at the edge of the colony one becomes surrounded by curious chicks. Eventually some of the chicks become overwhelmed by curiosity, and start pecking boot laces, trousers and hair to see what these strange humans are all about. Eventually they started climbing on our laps, which was just the kind of interaction that Paramount Pictures wanted for their documentary.

The sound recordist, Tony, had a large fluffy cover for his microphone that acted as a wind muffler, and by adding feet, wings and a beak he turned the microphone into a reasonably good imitation of a King penguin chick. Several chicks approached the microphone unsure of what to make of it. The effect was enhanced by Tony's ability to move it along on the telescopic boom.

Despite the humorous moments, and the things which did not go according to plan, the end result of the filming was very professional. They took over 30 hours of footage, and produced three separate documentaries of very high quality. The first, entitled "Rock on Penguins" covered my research into the decline of Rockhopper and Magellanic penguins. The second, entitled "Wind beneath their Wings", covered my albatross work, and the last one, entitled "Little Kings" was dedicated entirely to the King penguins. The programmes were shown world-wide on the Discovery Channel over three consecutive weeks. It was one of the proudest moments of my life.

Two weeks after the film crew left, Elena went into hospital. She had begun complaining of severe abdominal pains, and these pains turned out to be the result of an ectopic pregnancy, which is when the embryo becomes lodged in the fallopian tube rather than the uterus. The growing embryo ruptured the fallopian tube, causing considerable pain, and the death of the faetus.

Ever since the chemotherapy I had received for cancer in 1994, I was unable to have children by natural means, so this raised the issue of how Elena could have become pregnant. After much discussion Elena finally admitted that she had been having an affair. I was absolutely gutted.

Elena explained that ever since she had arrived in the Falklands as my wife she had been told by the police, government officials, newspaper articles, her friends, parents of her son's school mates, and just about everybody she met, that I was a convicted burglar who would shortly be kicked out of the Falklands, leaving her and her son homeless. Led to believe that her husband was a criminal, and fearing that she would shortly be left to fend for herself in a strange country, she had begun having an affair. When my innocence had finally been proven Elena had realised that she had believed the wrong people and had broken off her affair, but by that time she had already become pregnant.

I still loved Elena, but I felt betrayed. This was not helped by Elena's refusal to name the man she had been seeing. I was quite convinced that her determination not to name her lover was an indication that he was either a close friend of mine, or somebody whom I knew well.

When Elena got back from hospital she was so depressed by what she had done, and the consequences for our marriage, that she locked herself in the bedroom and refused to see anybody. Several of her friends phoned asking to speak to her, and I was forced to tell them that she did not wish to speak to anyone, leading to rumour and suspicion. A couple of days later there was a tremendous banging on the door. It was Lucy, one of Elena's friends. Lucy told me that she had heard that Elena had been in hospital, and demanded to see Elena to make sure that I had not been beating her or holding her prisoner in the house. I escorted her into the bedroom where Elena was still in bed, and left the two of them to chat. Elena again confessed to what she had done.

Lucy apologised to me for the accusations she had made, presumably expecting me to say that it was all okay. I told her I excepted her apology, but added that anybody entering my house making such accusations could no longer be considered a friend. I told her that she was no longer welcome in the house, and told her to leave.

Elena stayed with me in the Falklands for several weeks, hoping that her son would eventually change his mind and return, and that I could forget about what she had done. It was clear that Juan would never return after the harassment and abuse he had suffered at the hands of the police, and Elena's infidelity had split our marriage apart. I still loved her, and wanted so much to forgive her, but the enduring sense of betrayal was like water freezing in the cracks of a boulder, splitting it apart from within. Eventually Elena returned to Chile to be with her son, and despite wishing I could undo what had happened, I knew it was for the best.

Alone once more I had only my penguin research to keep me from loneliness and despair. I published my first book entitled "Penguins of the Falkland Islands and South America", which put down in writing virtually every bit of knowledge that I had learned during 7 years of penguin research. I also began work on my PhD thesis. But any thoughts that the Falkland Islands Government would let sleeping dogs lie after the British press had exposed their attempts to frame me, were soon dashed.

First I was told by the Falkland Islands Government that they were not going to renew my research permit because my work overlapped with government funded research. Then I received a phone call from the Attorney General, David Lang, to say that Executive Council had held another meeting to discuss my residency, and that they had refused it on the grounds that I "did not possess a knowledge or skill of which the Falklands were in need". Lang reminded me that up until now I had only been entitled to remain in the Falklands by virtue of my government post in the power station, but he said that a new law had just been introduced to take away that right. He told me I had three months to leave.

The reason I had kept my government employment in the power station alongside my penguin research was because it was the only thing which had given me a legal right to remain in the Falklands. Now the Falkland Islands Government had blocked my research permit, refused my application for permanent residency status, changed the law to take away my temporary residency status, and given me notice of deportation.

The timing of Lang's phone call could not have been more appropriate. It came just two days before I flew to La Serena in Chile, to present my penguin research at the 4th International Penguin Conference, and to launch my new book entitled "*Penguins of the Falkland*

Islands and South America". The irony and absurdity of the situation was not lost on the people attending the conference. The Falkland Islands Government could not have sent a clearer message about the value they placed on the protection of penguins.

Representatives of all the major penguin protection organisations from around the world were buying signed copies of my penguin book like they were hot cakes, whilst the Falkland Islands Government, who were responsible for managing the most important penguin breeding site in South America, were deporting me on the grounds that my knowledge and skills in penguin research and protection were of no value. This was seen by the participants of the conference as a declaration of the Falklands' complete disregard for penguin protection.

This message was re-enforced by Elena, who attended the conference with me. She told the participants how the Falkland Islands Government and Falkland Islands Police had deliberately stirred up harassment against her 9 year old son, in an attempt to try and force us to leave. One particularly poignant comment she made was that despite having lived through the Pinochet regime, she considered the Falklands to be the most corrupt place she had ever lived. Even Pinochet had drawn the line at targeting children.

Throughout the conference I was swept off my feet by support from the 120 participants. At the end of the 5 days of presentations, we began a two day workshop to discuss ways of protecting penguin populations world-wide. Threats against penguins were examined on a species by species basis, and a number of protection measures were proposed. The participants unanimously agreed that large-scale commercial fishing should be prohibited within 30 miles of penguin breeding sites in the Falkland Islands.

When I arrived back in the Falklands, the Falkland Islands Government had already received widespread condemnation for their refusal to protect penguins, and for their decision to deport me. The Attorney General phoned me to complain that I had discussed the issue of my deportation at the Penguin Conference, but he still insisted that I had to leave. On 2nd October he even put Executive Council's decision in writing. There was no right of appeal. He stated that I had three months from the date of the letter to take the matter to the Supreme Court before I would be deported. That gave me until January 2001.

The Falkland Islands Government had made it very clear that they were never going to let sleeping dogs lie, and that they would only be happy when they finally forced me out of the islands, by whatever means they felt they could get away with. The only thing on my side was that I was in the right. The Falkland Islands Government did not care about that, but they were concerned about the situation being publicised. The Attorney General's reaction to my discussing it at the penguin conference had shown that. I therefore decided to fight back using the only weapon I had - the truth, and lots of it.

The first thing I did was publicise the whole sorry saga on the Internet, using the "www.falklands.net" domain name which I had purchased. Within a few days of posting the story on the Internet, the Chief Executive of the Falkland Islands wrote to me asking for a right of reply on the web site. I agreed to his request on condition that he reciprocated this right of reply, by allowing me to answer the allegations made against me by the Falkland Islands Government in 1998; the very accusations that had led to the original suspension of my residency. In order for the Falkland Islands Government to grant me this right of reply, they would have had to reveal the details of the allegations, thereby exposing the corruption that had occurred. Needless to say the Chief Executive never replied.

Then I wrote to the press outlining everything that had happened, causing the government serious embarrassment. Following an article in the local newspaper, Penguin News, the Attorney General backed down on his threat to deport me, and even renewed my research license. The Attorney General felt the need to publicise this decision through a personal letter to the press, demonstrating the motives for such a U-turn. To my mind this was proof that his attempts to deport me had been illegal, and nothing short of government bullying. Had the government's attempts to deport me been legal and honourable, they would not have humiliated themselves by backing down.

In March 2001, the British Government came to my aid by offering me annual funding to conduct my penguin monitoring programme on an official footing. The Chilean government also invited me to set up a long-term penguin monitoring programme on Magdalena Island, and issued me with Chilean citizenship, in case I was eventually evicted from the

Falklands. In 2003 the Argentine government also invited me to include the huge colony at Cabo Virgenes into my penguin monitoring programme. With the backing of three governments, the Falkland Islands Government were no longer able to dismiss my work so easily, and found themselves increasingly isolated as the only government not to recognise the need for penguin protection.

CHAPTER SEVENTEEN

In 2002 the Spheniscus Penguin Conservation Workshop Report was finally published, sponsored by Sea World and the International Union for the Conservation of Nature (IUCN). It summarised the penguin protection measures deemed necessary by 43 penguin research organisations and 124 other conservation organisations, at the 4th International Penguin Conference and the Spheniscus Penguin Conservation Workshop. As such it represented the combined views and recommendations of the world's experts in the field of penguin research and conservation.

It stated that the Falklands was failing in its duty to protect penguins from commercial fishing, and outlined what was required of the Falkland Islands Government to rectify the problem. The report called for "*action against harvesting down the food web through industrial fishing*", and specified exactly what action was needed in the Falklands by saying:

"Recommend that there be no inshore fisheries within 30 miles of the coast in the Falklands. Restrict industrial fishing from areas of known concentrated penguin use at sea, including wintering and foraging areas for fledglings. Argentina and Falklands should establish an integrated series of marine reserves and zones to benefit all species of fish, seabirds and marine mammals".

The response by the Falkland Islands Government was predictable. Just as the Charity Commission had been powerless to prevent Falklands Conservation from rigging their elections, just as the Police Complaints Authority and Interpol had been powerless to bring the Falkland Islands Police to task for fabricating evidence, the scientific community was now powerless to force the Falkland Islands Government to protect penguins. The Falkland Islands Government was independent in every sense of the world. Financially and politically independent from Britain, they were not answerable to anybody, and not willing to concede any ground on issues that impacted on their ability to make huge amounts of money from commercial fishing.

For 11 years my ex-employers, Falklands Conservation, had raised money using the slogan "donate money and help us protect penguins". And yet in all that time neither Falklands Conservation nor the Falkland Islands Government had introduced one single measure to protect penguins from commercial fishing. They had undertaken research to give the impression of activity, but had done absolutely nothing to actually protect penguins. Conservation in the Falklands had become a front; a means of deflecting criticism away from commercial fishing which was making them rich, and on to bogus theories such as global population declines, global warming, drop in ocean temperatures, red tide, alien abduction - anything except commercial fishing.

For government officials and Falklands Conservation trustees, with major investments in commercial fishing companies, it was inconceivable to think that thousands of fishing boats scooping up fish and squid could in any way be linked to the starvation of penguins. There simply had to be a more complicated explanation.

Instead of tackling the effects of commercial fishing, Falklands Conservation concentrated on beach clean-ups, campaign leaflets to protect albatross in Uruguay, and the designation of a remote mountain range as a National Park. By designating a remote mountain that was under no threat from anyone, the Falkland Islands Government and Falklands Conservation were able to brag about the work they were doing to protect wildlife, work that in reality was little more than window dressing.

Whilst carrying out these projects, Falklands Conservation voted against a request by Birdlife International to designate Beauchene Island as a World Heritage site, because such designation was conditional upon the establishment of a no-fishing zone to protect the penguins! So much for the slogan 'help us protect penguins'. People donating money to Falklands Conservation should ask to see the minutes of the committee meeting which voted on this issue. Most of the Falklands Conservation trustees involved in making that decision had financial investments in commercial fishing and oil development, but not in Hill Cove Mountain.

With such a history it was perhaps no surprise that the Falkland Islands Government's official response to the Spheniscus Penguin Conservation Workshop Report, was to say that it did not apply to the Falklands because there was no industrial fishing taking place in the Falklands.

The Falkland Islands Government stated publicly that in their opinion the phrase "industrial fishing" only referred to the capture of fish and squid for grinding down into fishmeal. They argued that since the fish and squid caught around the Falklands was used for direct human consumption, rather than for processing into fishmeal, that they were not carrying out "industrial fishing", and were not bound by the recommendations of the report. This ridiculous statement was made by John Barton, the Director of Fisheries for the Falkland Islands Government, and published on the front page of Penguin News on 20th September 2002.

The statement was complete nonsense, and an insult to the body of international penguin experts who had spent two years preparing the report. The phrase "industrial fishing" simply referred to the activities of the fishing industry. It made no difference to the penguins whether their food was taken away for human consumption or for processing into fishmeal. But even disregarding any dispute over the phrase "industrial fishing", the report went on to say *"Recommend that there be no inshore fisheries within 30 miles of the coast in the Falklands"*. There is no ambiguity in this statement. It was a clear statement from the world's leading penguin experts, that the Falklands needed to protect penguins from commercial fishing through the establishment of no-fishing zones.

Since the Falkland Islands Government had made it clear that they were going to ignore the recommendations of the report, the International Penguin Conference organisers helped me to publish the findings of my penguin research in Chile's most prestigious peer-reviewed scientific journal, the Chilean Journal of Natural History. My manuscript was entitled *"The decline of Falkland Islands penguins in the presence of a commercial fishing industry"*. It presented overwhelming scientific evidence that penguin populations in the Falklands had declined by 90% since the establishment of commercial fishing, due to the starvation of penguins and their chicks caused by removal of their prey. It compared the Falklands to nearby Chile and Argentina, where penguin populations had remained healthy thanks to the establishment of no-fishing zones around penguin colonies.

Rockhopper penguins around the Falkland Islands had numbered 2,500,000 breeding pairs according to a British government survey published in 1984 (Croxall, McInnes and Prince 1984 *"The status and conservation of seabirds at the Falkland Islands"*, ICBP Technical Publication No.2, British Antarctic Survey, Cambridge). The Falkland Islands fishing industry was officially commissioned three years later in 1987, and by the year 2000, Rockhopper penguin numbers had crashed by 90% to just 250,000 breeding pairs according to Falklands Conservation's own census figures.

On nearby Staten Island in Argentina, Rockhopper penguin populations had increased at such a rate that it was impossible to explain the increase from breeding success alone. The only way to explain the rapid population increase on Staten Island was through massive immigration of Rockhoppers from elsewhere, and the only site big enough to be the source of such immigration was the Falkland Islands. Rockhopper penguins had moved from the Falkland Islands to Argentina by the thousand, presumably because fish and squid were more plentiful in Argentina as a result of the Falklands' indiscriminate commercial fishing.

The other penguin species which had declined dramatically in the Falklands was the Magellanic penguin. The nearest Magellanic penguin colonies to the Falklands were the Magdalena-Contramaestra Islands in Chile, and Cabo Virgenes in Argentina. Again, whilst populations had crashed by 90% in the Falklands following the onset of commercial fishing, Magellanic penguin populations in nearby Chile and Argentina had increased.

The Magdalena-Contramaestra Islands lie in the Straits of Magellan near the city of Punta Arenas in southern Chile, just 500 kilometres from the Falklands. The population of Magellanic penguins on these islands in the early 1990s was around 50,000 breeding pairs according to Chilean government surveys. My research at these sites, conducted on behalf of the Chilean government, demonstrated that this had increased by over 70% to around 87,000 breeding pairs by 2002.

Similarly in Argentina, a population census in the 1990s had recorded a population total of 90,000 breeding pairs at Cabo Virgenes, but this had since increased to 120,000 breeding pairs by 2003, whilst the Falkland Islands population just 400 kilometres away had crashed due to the annual starvation of chicks.

Magdalena Island Penguin Census November 2002

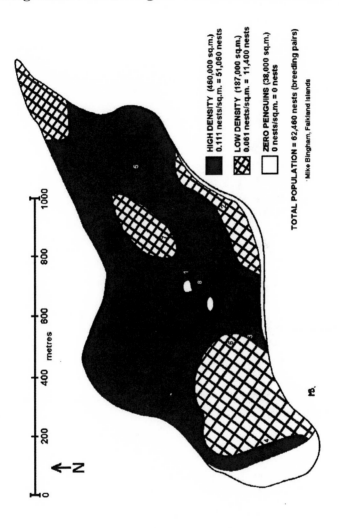

Contramaestra Island Penguin Census November 2002

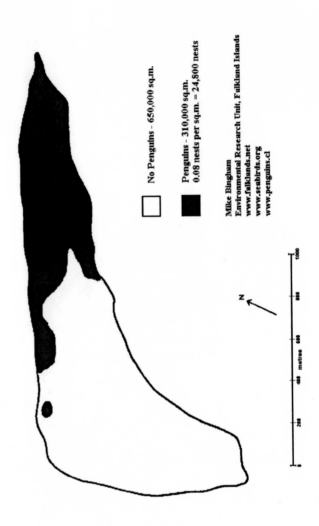

No Penguins – 650,000 sq.m.

Penguins – 310,000 sq.m.
0.08 nests per sq.m. = 24,800 nests

Mike Bingham
Environmental Research Unit, Falkland Islands
www.falklands.net
www.seabirds.org
www.penguins.cl

N

0   200   400 metres 600   800   1000

Cabo Virgenes Penguin Census November 2003

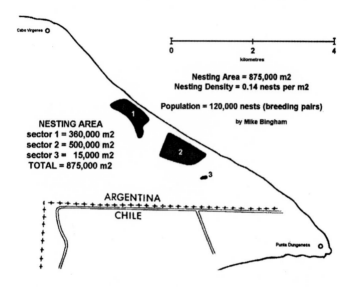

So what was the difference between the increasing colonies in Chile and Argentina, and the declining colonies in the adjacent Falklands? The difference was that these colonies in Chile and Argentina were all protected by no-fishing zones that prevented commercial fishing boats from depleting fish and squid stocks close to penguin colonies. However this had not always been the case.

Many years earlier, commercial fishing had taken place around the Magdalena-Contramaestra Islands, and penguin populations had declined as a result, just like in the Falklands. Then the Chilean government had declared the area a nature reserve, and established a no-fishing zone around the islands, since when penguin populations had almost doubled. The reason why no-fishing zones worked so well was not hard to explain.

Since 1997 I had been comparing penguin populations in the Falklands with Chile and Argentina. In Chile and Argentina, where no-fishing zones protected penguin colonies from commercial fishing, Magellanic penguins found food for their chicks in 8 to 14 hours. As a result chicks were fed daily, so chicks were well nourished, so chick survival was high, and chicks were in good condition when they fledged, giving them the best chance of survival. A penguin that survives its first few months of life, as it learns how to catch food on its own aided only by its fat reserves, will probably go on to live to be 20 years of age.

However in the Falklands, where commercial fishing was permitted close to penguin colonies, adult penguins found it harder to find fish and squid, which were less abundant due to the huge amounts being taken commercially. So adult penguins took an average of 35 hours to find food for their chicks, so chicks were fed less than half that of chicks in Chile and Argentine, so most chicks died from starvation each year.

An additional problem was that Magellanic penguins unable to find sufficient fish and squid, would feed their chicks crustaceans, which are very indigestible for chicks. Presumably adult penguins consider it better to feed their chicks crustaceans than to return with empty stomachs, but whilst a few are not harmful, chicks cannot survive on a diet of crustaceans.

With chicks in the Falklands receiving less than half the amount of food, much of which was of a type that was indigestible to chicks, it was not surprising that most of the Magellanic penguin chicks in the Falklands starved to death every year. In Chile and Argentina an average of 1.4 chicks per nest survived each year, whilst in the Falklands it was less than 0.5 chicks per nest, with most chicks starving in February, long after they should have fledged and left the nest. Those chicks that did eventually fledge in the Falklands were too underweight to have any real chance of surviving their first few weeks of life, weighing an average of just 2.6 kilograms, compared to 3.4 kilograms in Chile and Argentina. So virtually no chicks were surviving to maturity in the Falklands to replace natural adult mortality.

In 1982, British troops sent to the Falklands were told they were liberating an island of 2,000 people and 6 million penguins, a figure supported by the British government's British Antarctic Survey report (Croxall, McInnes and Prince 1984 "*The status and conservation of seabirds at the Falkland Islands*", ICBP Technical Publication No.2, British Antarctic Survey, Cambridge). The 6 million penguins that inhabited the islands in 1982 had crashed to just 1 million by 2002 - the loss of five million penguins!

Research from around the world has shown that Rockhopper and Magellanic penguins generally forage within 30 kilometres of their colony whilst rearing chicks, unless a depletion of resources forces them to forage further afield. Hence the international call for no-fishing zones around penguin colonies.

In May 2002, as if to underline the dispute now raging over penguin protection, conditions became so bad around the Falklands that adult penguins started dying of starvation by the thousand. Beaches around the Falklands were littered with the corpses of over

100,000 dead penguins. A few of the corpses were sent to the government Veterinary Department by concerned landowners for analysis, and autopsies confirmed that the penguins had been reduced to skin and bone by starvation, with no traces of food in their stomachs.

Nidia Mendez and I went to look at the scale of the problem, and we were appalled by what we saw. On Saunders Island, where Paramount Pictures had filmed the documentary about my work three years earlier, the beaches was littered with dead penguins. Some were fresh, some partially decayed with bones protruding. All had died within the previous few weeks, and all had died during their annual moult. Their condition and weight showed that they had died as a result of starvation. A few starving Gentoo penguins were still alive, still moulting their feathers, but too weak to even walk, or to ever return to the sea to find food. Vultures and Caracaras hung around them waiting for them to die.

We did a count just along the short section of beach at The Neck, and counted a total of 2,067 dead Rockhopper penguins and 509 dead Gentoo penguins. The 2,067 dead Rockhoppers came from a colony of 8,000 adults, so the corpses actually found and counted amounted to more than a quarter of the entire colony. For each corpse found and counted, there must have been at least one other buried in the sand, covered by kelp, or washed out to sea, so at least 50% of the entire colony had actually died.

The penguins had starved to death because they had been unable to find enough food to build up body fat reserves prior to their annual moult. When penguins change their feathers, they loose their insulation, making it impossible to enter the icy cold ocean to feed for at least three weeks. Penguins therefore rely on fat and protein reserves built up prior to the moult, in order to see them through this period of enforced fasting.

During the moult period they not only need fat reserves to keep warm, but also fat and protein to synthesise a complete new set of feathers. If they are unable to build up fat and protein reserves during February and March, because food is too scarce, then they starve. Without enough fat reserves to survive the moult they are doomed, like a car setting out on a journey without enough petrol. When the fuel runs out, the motor stops, and the penguin dies.

Some of the landowners managed to save a few of the penguins by feeding them fish and squid to build up their strength, further proof that starvation was the one and only cause of death. If toxic poisoning or disease had been the cause of death, then simply providing food would not have resulted in a 100% recovery rate.

The same thing had occurred in 1986, when hundreds of thousands of Rockhopper penguins had starved to death during their annual moult - exactly the same as had occurred now in 2002. The 1986 starvation had been blamed on uncontrolled commercial fishing. It had led to government promises of control measures over commercial fishing, and the establishment of the Seabird Monitoring Programme, the very programme which I had built up during my employment with Falklands Conservation.

Unfortunately the controls over commercial fishing that had been promised were subsequently designed to ensure the financial sustainability of squid and fish stocks, rather than to protect wildlife that competed with the fishing industry for food. The target for squid catches had been set at 60% of the entire biomass each and every year, leaving just 40% for penguins, seabirds and seals, plus the following year's breeding stock. As for the Seabird Monitoring Programme, the election of oil company directors and fishing company owners as trustees of Falklands Conservation, had meant that any evidence of conflict between commercial fishing and wildlife was being well and truly buried.

Ever since 1986, regret had been expressed that no conservation body had existed in the Falklands at the time to look into the 1986 mass starvation event. Now in 2002, Falklands Conservation was a well-staffed conservation organisation receiving nearly £200,000 (US$300,000) per annum from the Falkland Islands Government. So you can imagine the public surprise when Falklands Conservation refused to send anybody out to investigate the beaches covered in dead penguins. Falklands Conservation stated that they had several key personnel away on annual leave, and had nobody available to look into the starvation of penguins.

Both Falklands Conservation and the Falkland Islands Government refused to send anybody out to investigate the disaster, and even prevented other people from conducting independent investigations. A veterinary surgeon from the University of Mar de Plata, with specialist skills in seabird mortality, came to the Falklands offering to assist, but he was told by Falklands Conservation that he could not analyse the corpses without a permit, and that the person responsible for issuing permits was away on annual leave!

With beaches littered with the corpses of over 100,000 Rockhopper penguins, a species that was listed as an endangered species, not one single government conservationist or official went out to investigate. The motive was clear. They already knew the cause, and did not wish to gather evidence which they would then need to cover up.

The Falkland Islands Government had control over fishing grounds which extended 300 kilometres from the coast, so the no-fishing zones requested by the world's penguin experts would have reduced the area over which fishing boats could operate by around 3%. The Falkland Islands Government were very wealthy, with an annual income of around £20,000 (US$30,000) for every man, woman and child living in the islands, an income that was almost entirely generated from commercial fishing, hence the reluctance to reduce the fishing area by 3% to protect penguins.

However a 3% reduction in fishing grounds would not have meant a 3% reduction in income or catch. On the contrary, as any population biologist would confirm, providing a "safe-haven" is a very good way of preventing accidental over-exploitation of target species through commercial fishing. The disadvantages of implementing such protection would have been minimal, whilst the gains would have been great in terms of wildlife protection, fisheries management, and international goodwill.

Chile and Argentina were both poor countries compared to the Falklands, but they had both taken measures to protect penguins from commercial fishing through the establishment of no-fishing zones. There was no reason, except greed, why the Falkland Islands Government did not adopt similar measures to protect Falklands penguins.

Whilst Falklands Conservation and the Falkland Islands Government were keen to do nothing, landowners and members of the public in the Falklands kept phoning me asking me to do something to draw attention to what was happening. So I contacted a couple of sources in the British media, and very soon the story hit the headlines around the world. On 9th June 2002 the Sunday Independent in Britain ran a full page story entitled *"The Plight of Falklands Starving Penguins"*, and this was followed by the BBC who broadcast the story world-wide on Radio and TV. Within a few days the story was on Radio and Television across the USA, Europe, and Canada, and by 27th September 2002, La Prensa Austral published the story across South America in an article entitled *"100 mil pingüinos mueren de hambre"*.

The Falklands newspaper, Penguin News, was flooded by overseas readers writing in to complain that the Falklands should be ashamed of allowing penguins to starve without providing protection from over-fishing. The British Foreign & Commonwealth Office also received a flood of complaints demanding that they take action against the Falkland Islands Government to force them to protect penguins.

The Falkland Islands Government realised that they had to act; the only question was what type of action to take. For greedy government officials with investments in commercial fishing, protecting penguins was simply not an option, which meant reverting back to Clifton's old policy - reduce the number of references to starving penguins by getting rid of the person blowing the whistle.

The following month I received a letter from the Falkland Islands Government saying that my right to remain in employment had again been revoked by a change in the law, and that I must leave at the end of December 2002 unless I could obtain residency status. This contradicted the promise the Attorney General, David Lang, had made two years earlier in his personal letter to Penguin News. The only way to avoid deportation was to obtain residency status, so I applied again. I received a letter from the Governor of the Falkland Islands, Howard Pierce, stating that Executive Council had refused to grant me residency status on the grounds that I had *"repeatedly sought to discredit and bring into disrepute the state of the Falkland Islands environment and the role of the Government in its protection"*.

This was an outrageous breach of the laws governing freedom of speech, which protected the rights of the citizen to criticise government without discrimination. I made an appointment to see the Governor, and told him that he must surely realise that he was acting illegally. I told him that unless he and Executive Council reconsidered their decision that I would take the matter to the press, and if necessary to the Supreme Court for violation of human rights. The Governor refused to make any comment. He listened to what I had to say, but made no reply.

Despite his failure to comment, my threats to the Governor must have caught the attention of somebody, because a few days later I received a phone call threatening to kill me if I spoke to the press. Again I did the only thing I could do and reported the threatening call to the police.

On the previous occasion that I had received malicious phonecalls, in February 1999, the Falkland Islands Police had put a Malicious Calls Interceptor on the line and caught the culprit. However they claimed to have accidentally lost the identity of the culprit by making an error when tracing the connection through the switchboard. I was quite convinced that having discovered that the culprit was a government employee, indeed a member of Customs & Immigration whose voice I had identified, that the police had deliberately lost the trace to prevent political embarrassment.

So this time I opted for a trace that used the civilian switchboard operator to identify the malicious caller, since they would be independent of the police, or so I thought. A few days later the caller once again threatened to kill me, and even told me that they were on their way to do it. I phoned the Falkland Islands Police, who contacted the switchboard operator, and the identity of the caller was established. The Falkland Islands Police sent an officer to arrest the culprit, and I waited for the outcome.

A few days later Inspector Len McGill phoned me to tell me that the Attorney General, David Lang, had decided not to proceed with a prosecution against the culprit. I was furious, and asked for an explanation. I was told that under Falklands law it was not illegal to threaten to kill somebody over the telephone. This was absolute nonsense, as any lawyer could confirm. If I had phoned Clifton or the Governor and threatened to kill them, my feet would not have touched the ground on my way out of the Falklands.

Since the Police were refusing to prosecute the individual, I asked Inspector McGill for the identity of the culprit, so that I would at least know who was threatening to kill me, in case they approached me on a dark night. Inspector McGill told me that the identity of the man who had threatened to kill me was confidential, and that it was not in the public interest to reveal his identity. So I contacted Cable & Wireless, the telephone company that had identified the caller, and asked them for the identity of the culprit.

Brian Summers, Manager of Cable & Wireless, and by coincidence also a trustee of Falklands Conservation, wrote to me stating: "*I am advised that I **cannot** reveal the identity of the malicious caller. All details relating to the call have been forwarded to the Police.*"

The Falkland Islands Police had sunk to an all time low. Not content with fabricating evidence in an attempt to deport me, and using convictions belonging to another person to harass me, they were now protecting the identity of somebody who had threatened to commit murder. I complained to the police in writing, but they only repeated in writing what they had already told me, that they had identified the person who had made the threats, had decided to drop the charges, and could not reveal the person's identity.

At the time that the caller had made his threat to kill me if I went to the press, the only person with whom I had discussed going to the press was the Governor. That, combined with the fact that the police were protecting the person threatening to kill me, convinced me that the culprit was somebody high up in government, somebody who simply could not be identified without an international scandal. There were clearly no limits to the moral depths to which the Falkland Islands Government and Falkland Islands Police were prepared to sink.

Once again I wrote to Dafydd Wigley MP, who had helped me expose the Falkland Islands Government in 1999. I also wrote to Liberty, Human Rights UK, the BBC, and a number of UK newspapers who had covered my story in 1999. Because the post office was part of the Falkland Islands Government, I decided to post these letters by registered mail, to ensure that they were not destroyed or tampered with prior to reaching their destination. It was impossible to keep the nature of my letters secret. The pile of letters to newspaper editors, human rights organisations and an MP naturally raised a few eyebrows in the post office.

I waited for a reply to my letters, but nothing came. A few weeks later I received an email from Dafydd Wigley saying that he had received my envelope, but that it had been opened and the documents were missing. I am sure he would not have written to acknowledge an envelope without any contents had he not already been familiar with the background to my case and become suspicious. When I made enquiries to the various newspapers and human rights organisations, I discovered that their letters had also either gone astray or had the documents removed, despite having a post office tracking number, and requiring signature upon delivery.

I complained to the post office, who initially said they would look into it. A few days later they told me there was nothing they could do, even though I had the registration certificates that should have allowed each of the letters to be tracked. For so many registered letters to different recipients to be opened or lost was too much of a coincidence. The post office was part of the Falkland Islands Government, and I now began to think that their influence permeated every aspect of Falklands society.

By now I had begun legal proceedings to take the Falkland Islands Government to the Supreme Court, and my solicitor advised me to hold off with the press until after the court case, when the matter would be settled one way or the other. If I won in court, then the press would have the evidence they needed to write a proper story, using the findings of the court rather than my unsubstantiated accusations.

In February 2003, Magellanic penguins were in a worse state than usual. Fish and squid stocks had still not recovered from the previous season, and adult penguins were finding it impossible to feed their chicks. Chick growth had been slowed down so much through malnutrition, that those chicks which had not actually starved to death, were still too small to fend for themselves, more than a month after the fat healthy chicks in Chile and Argentina had left the nest.

Adult penguins have an internal body clock which tells them when they need to stop caring for chicks, in order to make their own preparations for surviving the winter. Feeding chicks is very demanding, and adult penguins loose weight during chick-rearing. Failure to abandon chicks that are taking too long to develop would lead to starvation of the adults during their moult. So the chicks, which if properly fed would have left the nest weeks before like in Chile and Argentina, were now abandoned by the adults and left to starve. Still in chick plumage, they were unable to go to sea to find food, and starvation was a certainty.

I contacted the Falkland Islands Government for permission to feed the orphaned chicks to prevent them starving, but the Environmental Planning Officer, under advice from Falklands Conservation, refused me permission. He said that Becky Ingham of Falklands Conservation had advised him to let nature take its course.

There are many occasions when conservationists must let nature take its course, but I viewed this situation in the same light as I had viewed the saving of buried hatchlings in Hawaii. If man, through greed and ignorance, creates a situation that is killing wildlife, then standing by and letting it happen is not nature taking its course. Since the annual abandonment and starvation of penguin chicks was largely the result of commercial fishing, then the only way to let nature take its course was to protect penguins from commercial fishing, something which neither Falklands Conservation nor the Falkland Islands Government were willing to do.

Having no respect whatsoever for either Falklands Conservation or the Falkland Islands Government, I ignored their ruling and went ahead and fed the chicks. I fed each chick once a day with between 500 and 800 grams of fish, and weighed each of the chicks daily to monitor their growth. At first I had to cut the fish into small pieces, and force the pieces down the chicks' throats until they swallowed, because they were not used to being fed by anyone except their parents. However within a couple of days the hungry chicks realised that they were being helped with much needed food, and began taking the fish on their own, making the process a lot easier.

Had the Falkland Islands Government caught me feeding the chicks against their wishes, I would have been prosecuted, but since the penguin colonies at Gypsy Cove and Hadassa Bay were well away from town, it was easy to do it without getting caught. My reward came when the chicks, now fat and healthy, finally fledged and took to the sea in late March and early April. Not one of these chicks would have survived if I had not intervened.

With dead penguins that had starved to death littering the beaches, and chicks being abandoned because adults could not find enough food to feed them, it was obvious that penguin populations were in trouble due to lack of food. It was also becoming increasingly clear that people tasked with protecting Falklands wildlife were more concerned in deflecting blame away from commercial fishing, in order to protect private investments in local fishing companies.

So when a handful of well-nourished penguins were found dead from no apparent cause, Falklands Conservation launched a major investigation. Whilst the starvation of a hundred thousand penguins the previous year had not been worthy of their investigation, the death of a handful of well-nourished penguins clearly was. Indeed for people trying to deflect criticism away from commercial fishing it was a gift from God.

Falklands Conservation presented an article for publication in New Scientist magazine, blaming the penguin deaths on a drop in ocean temperature, even though drops in ocean temperature were normally beneficial to penguins. The New Scientist is not a peer-reviewed publication, so they accepted the article for publication without asking for evidence to support the theory. However shortly before publication Falklands Conservation changed their minds and began blaming the penguin deaths on red tide, a natural phenomenon which occurs when algal blooms create toxins that enter the food chain through filter-feeding animals such as shellfish. Not surprisingly New Scientist dropped Falklands Conservation like a hot potato. Presumably they realised that responsible researchers do not present scientific discoveries for publication, only to turn round the following week asking to change it for a different theory.

A serious problem with the red tide theory was that toxins only accumulate to dangerous levels in filter-feeding invertebrates such as shellfish, or animals that eat shellfish, such as humans. Penguins do not eat shellfish, but the people of the Falklands do. It was therefore hard for the red tide theory to explain how penguins which did not eat shellfish could have died, whilst people eating shellfish had not even become ill. Chile and Argentina had suffered out-breaks of red tide for years, and people had often become ill as a result, but the penguins there had never been affected because they simply don't eat the type of filter-feeding invertebrates which become contaminated with red tide.

Not content with blaming red tide for the death of a handful of well-fed penguins, Falklands Conservation now began implying that the May 2002 mass starvation of penguins had also been due to red tide, thereby justifying the government's decision not to establish no-fishing zones. This was nothing short of a lie. The 100,000 dead penguins which had littered the beaches in May 2002 had been reduced to skin and bone through lack of food. Autopsies had shown these penguins to have empty stomachs. Landowners had saved some of them just by feeding them. Indeed it would have been impossible for penguins moulting on the beach to have ingested red tide toxins, because they are unable to enter the sea to feed during their moult. There was no doubt that these penguins had died from starvation, brought about by their inability to find food prior to the moult, just like the penguin chicks which were starving to death each and every year, such as the ones I had saved by feeding.

Seeking independent confirmation that red tide could not have been the cause of the May 2002 starvation, I wrote to Dr Stephen Bates of the Fisheries and Oceans Centre in New Brunswick, Canada. Dr Bates was an expert on Phytoplankton toxins and red tides, and he stated "*If the stomachs were empty, then it is unlikely that the penguins consumed food contaminated with domoic acid. When seabird and marine mammal deaths are attributed to domoic acid, the toxic diatom Pseudo-*

nitzschia australis and domoic acid can be found in the stomachs."

This is hardly surprising. People who die from eating something poisonous have remains of the poisoned food in their stomachs. People who die with stomachs completely empty have been without food for a long time, and have therefore died from causes other than eating poisoned food.

Dr Michelle Powers, a marine biologist specialising in disease and mortality with the Gulf Fisheries Centre, was also of the same opinion, stating "*if I had many dead animals with empty stomachs my conclusion would be that they had not eaten in some time. I would consider availability of resources*".

The report by the Government Veterinary Officer, Kevin Lawrence, following autopsy of the dead penguins from May 2002, had stated that the stomachs of the dead penguins had been empty. There was therefore nothing in the stomachs of the penguins from May 2002 to have caused red tide poisoning, confirming that this mass starvation was not caused by red tide, or any other poisoning, but by lack of food.

Falklands Conservation clearly understood this, but were presumably more interested in deflecting criticism away from commercial fishing than they were in protecting the environment - just as they had previously blamed penguin declines on a global trend - just as they had lied about oil spills occurring outside Falklands waters - just as they had initially blamed the death of penguins on a drop in ocean temperature - just as they had made false allegations to try and deport me, allegations which they had been forced to admit in writing had been untrue.

Whilst all this was going on, a member of Falklands Conservation's staff was arrested, prosecuted and sent to prison for two years, for embezzling £40,000 (US$60,000) of charity money - money which had been donated for wildlife protection!

CHAPTER EIGHTEEN

I had engaged a British lawyer to fight my case against the Falkland Islands Government, in order to ensure that they could not be 'got at' by the labyrinth of corruption that permeated Falklands society. It was a sad fact that virtually every part of Falklands society was in some way run or controlled by the Falkland Islands Government. Apart from the obvious control of police, immigration, work permits and building permits, the Falkland Islands Government also ran many other departments that in other societies would be independent, such as the post office, newspaper office and radio station. It was imperative that my legal representation was based outside the Falklands where they would be free from intimidation, even though this made my legal fees very expensive.

My British lawyer, Maya Lester, had been engaged through Ledingham Chalmers, who also engaged Rory Gilchrist to act as my local legal representative. He was in the Falklands only until the end of the trial, so nobody within the Falkland Islands Government could manipulate him through threats concerning his career or residency status. One of the first things that my legal team did was demand the release of key documents, and these included the documents which the police had held secret since 1999 in their case file. These documents were handed over, and proved that Falklands Conservation had lied in an attempt to frame me.

The secretary of Falklands Conservation, Carol (Hay) Miller, had made a statement to the Falkland Islands Police dated 31st March 1999 in which she wrote "*I cannot recall at any time during the interview the panel being made aware by Mr Bingham that he did not hold the relevant degree for that post, nor can I recollect ANY arrangements being made by ANY of the panel to arrange ANY exams to be held in the Falkland Islands following Mr Bingham's appointment as Conservation Officer*".

In this statement Mrs Miller not only denied any knowledge of arranging transport to my exams after my employment, but even denied any knowledge of my having taken any exams. Indeed this denial was of paramount importance to the entire case against me, since knowledge of my exams would have meant Falklands Conservation knew all along that I had not completed my Open University course, thereby destroying their accusation that I had lied about finishing my course.

However in the very same case file the Falkland Islands Police had held my letter to Mrs Miller dated 8th August 1993 in which I had written "*I have made arrangements to take my Open University Examination at RAF Mount Pleasant on 21st October*". The Police file also contained Mrs Miller's reply dated 15th September 1993, in which she acknowledged receipt of my letter, and replied "*It shouldn't be a problem getting you to MPA on 21st October for your examination*".

Mrs Miller, Dr John Croxall and Julian Fitter had all made sworn statements to the Falkland Islands Police denying knowledge of these exams, exams which Mrs Miller's letter proved they had known about all along. The whole accusation of deception which the Falkland Islands Police had tried to bring against me in 1999 was based on these false statements. I would never have even been arrested if Mrs Miller's letter been discovered earlier, which is presumably why the Falkland Islands Police had subsequently kept it secret and denied its existence, even to the point of stating in writing that no such letter had been found during their investigation.

Furious at how people I had once worked with had made false statements to the police in an attempt to frame me, I deposited copies of these police statements and letters in the public library, so that everyone could see for themselves how these respected pillars of society had behaved.

Some members of Executive Council began to realise that their actions were not going to stand up to close scrutiny, and Councillor John Birmingham approached me offering to reverse the decision to kick me out if I halted my Supreme Court proceedings. He called me to a meeting in the Councillors Chambers on 7th April 2003, and told me to instruct my solicitor to halt the court proceedings in exchange for help in securing permanent residency rights. He added that I must send a copy of these instructions to the Attorney General, David Lang, so that Executive Council would know that I had halted the court proceedings, otherwise they would not reverse their decision to kick me out.

I did as I was instructed. I wrote to my legal representatives asking them to halt the court proceedings, stating the reasons that I wanted them to do so, and asking them to copy these instructions to the Attorney General as requested. Executive Council held their meeting, and offered to allow me to stay in my employment until the end of 2004. The fact that they were able to make such an offer proved that their attempts to kick me out in the first place had been illegal. Executive Council were not empowered to rewrite the law if the law had really stated I must leave.

However a temporary postponement of my deportation from the Falklands was of no use to me, and was not the right to residency which I had been promised, so I rejected Executive Council's offer and resumed legal proceedings against them.

The court hearing was to take place in the Supreme Court, and was to be a major event, challenging as it did the Falkland Islands Government's right to silence people who spoke out against them, through withdrawal of residency and work permits, police harassment and other unconstitutional behaviour. The Falkland Islands Government were forced by the court to release documents relating to the decision making process, including minutes of meetings and personal correspondence. This documentation revealed some outrageous and corrupt behaviour within government.

A letter dated 24th May 1998 from Councillor Lewis Clifton to the Environmental Planning Officer read "*I am advised that Mr Bingham wrote to your offices in March of this year undertaking to provide a coastline survey of East Falkland. I must ask you to refrain from engaging the services of Mr Bingham.*" Councillor Clifton was at that time a member of Executive Council, empowering him to make this demand, but the demand was made as Chairman of Falklands Conservation on Falklands Conservation headed paper. For a member of Executive Council to use his position to prevent work being given to a competitor of an organisation which he represented as a private citizen, was a breach of power, and should have resulted in dismissal under British law.

The minutes of the 22nd February 2001 Executive Council meeting recorded how one Councillor had suggested that my views on wildlife protection were the result of a "*medical problem*"!

Councillors had then discussed how they could get rid of me, and had turned to the Attorney General asking if there were any legal means of doing so. The Attorney General had replied that there were not, since the law prevented them from getting rid of me just because of my views. He told Executive Council members that "*Mr Bingham's comments are permitted under the Constitutional provisions regarding freedom of speech.*"

Councillor John Birmingham had stated that he had originally supported my right to live in the Falklands, until I had told the International Penguin Conference about the decline in Falklands penguins, after which he had decided I must be got rid of.

The Chief Executive, Michael Blanch, had stated *"This would not be a wise move in view of the recent keen interest shown in Mr Bingham's case by the journalists from the Mail on Sunday. It would be better to wait until after the journalists have published the articles arising from their visit."*

The minutes of the 22nd February 2001 Executive Council meeting concluded *"Council decided that before taking any further action there was a need to monitor what the journalists who had recently visited might publish in the UK newspapers regarding Mr Bingham's case."*

These were the official minutes of discussions between the Falkland Islands Government's highest officials - The Governor, the Chief Executive, the Attorney General, and the elected members of Executive Council. That these comments had been recorded in the minutes of Executive Council meetings, and distributed throughout the Falkland Islands Government, demonstrated how these people believed themselves to be above the law. I could only speculate on what had been said off the record, in private discussions, where matters such as using the police to arrest me, the harassment of my family, and the threats against my life had been discussed.

Following the release of these documents it became clear that the Falkland Islands Government's behaviour was indefensible in a court of law, and that they were going to loose big style. Councillors and government officials, fearful of the consequences, began offering me compromises to halt the court proceedings, but now that these documents had come to light I knew I was going to win, and was not prepared to halt the proceedings. I wanted the world to know what they had done.

On 31st July 2003 the Directional Hearing took place, which laid out the timetable for the court hearing that was to take place in October. During September I sorted through my personal belongings in preparation for leaving the Falklands if things did not go well in court. On 28th September I sold many of my possessions in the flea market in the Town Hall. I also dumped a lot of other items on the rubbish tip. I was confident that my legal arguments were valid, but was still concerned that the Supreme Court hearing was to be held in the Falklands, where it might have been subjected to intimidation from the Falkland Islands Government. By now my projected legal fees were around £20,000 (US$30,000), and if I lost the case it was likely that the court would also order me to pay the Falkland Islands Government's legal costs as well, which were even higher. The stakes were high. I risked financial ruin if I lost.

However my main fear was not losing the case, but rather the ruthless behaviour that these powerful people would resort to rather than face public disgrace and criminal charges. With much less motive than they now had, they had previously resorted to breaking into my house, planting evidence, fabricating documents, accusing me of false crimes, committing perjury, threatening to kill me and sabotaging my car. I could not rule out the possibility that they would make another last ditch attempt to frame me for something really serious, or even possibly carry out their threat to kill me. I therefore made plans to seek protection in the one place where I knew the Falkland Islands Government's long arm of corruption could not reach - Argentina.

As a consequence of the bitter dispute between the Falklands and Argentina, which had raged since the 1982 war, I knew that even the highest officials within the Falkland Islands Government would not be able to use their influence against me in Argentina. It is ironic that for so many years the Falkland Islands Government had claimed the moral high-ground over Argentina in terms of political morality and democracy, and now the Falkland Islands Government was about to be exposed in the Supreme Court for high-level corruption and abuse of human rights, whilst I sought safety in Argentina, a country whose political morality was something which the Falklands could only dream of. The British servicemen who gave their lives to uphold democracy in the Falklands in the 1982 war, would have turned in their graves if they could have seen where their sacrifice was to have led.

On 17th October I attended court to swear in my final affidavit, and left the remainder of the court hearing in the hands of my legal team. On Saturday 18th October 2003 I took the flight to Rio Gallegos in Argentina, where I would await the outcome of the court hearing under the protection of Argentine justice.

On 20th October I met with Argentine officials from the Consejo Agrario Provincial, and was taken to the penguin colony at Cabo Virgenes, where I began conducting a population census for the Argentine government. Nobody except for a few Argentine officials knew where I was, not even my legal team, who thought I was in Chile. It was the only way I felt safe. I kept in touch with my lawyers using the telephone at the Argentine Navy station at Cabo Virgenes, knowing full well that these calls could not be traced. This paranoia turned out to be well founded. My careful planning foiled a last-ditch attempt to frame me for drugs, which unbeknown to me had been planted in my house shortly before I left the Falklands.

My time spent working at Cabo Virgenes was not wasted, and proved more fruitful than I could have imagined. Unlike the Falkland Islands Government, the Argentine government were keen to protect penguins, and Cabo Virgenes already had a no-fishing zone around the penguin colony. My census recorded a population total of 120,000 breeding pairs, which was a 33% increase over the previous population census of 90,000 breeding pairs conducted in the 1990s. The increase was due to good management, combined with protection against commercial fishing: stark contrast to the nearby Falkland Islands, where greed and the refusal to protect penguins had resulted in a 90% decline over the same period.

Chief Justice James Wood presided over the Supreme Court hearings, flown down 14,000 kilometres from Britain especially for my court case. My lawyer, Maya Lester, also flew down from Britain. She was assisted by Rory Wilson of Ledingham Chalmers. The Falkland Islands Government also flew down a team of top lawyers from Britain. No expense was spared. The stakes were high and so were the legal fees.

The Governor of the Falkland Islands, Howard Pierce, defended his position by claiming that even though he had stated in writing that he had refused my right to residency because I had "*repeatedly sought to discredit and bring into disrepute the state of the Falkland Islands environment and the role of the Government in its protection*", that this reason had not actually played a part in his mind when considering the matter. He said that he had realised that they were not relevant and appropriate grounds for refusal, but had stated them because Executive Council had told him to.

Executive Council shifted the blame back onto the Governor by saying that although they had recommended refusing my right to live in the Falklands on those grounds, the overall responsibility for making the final decision had lain with the Governor. It was after all he who had signed the letter putting such reasons in writing. The Supreme Court then heard how:

1) My residency rights had been suspended by Executive Council five years earlier, following false allegations of data theft by Councillor Lewis Clifton, acting as a member of Executive Council, Director of Desire Petroleum and Chairman of Falklands Conservation

2) Falklands Conservation and Executive Council had been subsequently forced to admit in writing that these allegations were untrue

3) I had been arrested and released by the Falkland Islands Police three times on the basis of falsified documents and false testimony

4) Falklands Conservation had made sworn statements to the Police accusing me of falsely claiming to have completed my university exams at the time of my interview, but the Police found a letter from Falklands Conservation offering me transport to my final exams, proving that they had lied in their statements

5) The Falkland Islands Police had denied the existence of this letter in writing, until they had been forced to hand it over by the Supreme Court four years later

6) The Falkland Islands Police had admitted using their own computer to print an alternative version of my job application form, and to changing the entries for my qualifications, before arresting me on the basis of the changes they themselves had made to the document

7) The Falkland Islands Police had deceived the public into believing that I had criminal convictions for burglary, after Interpol had made it clear that I did not, forcing my 9 year old stepson to leave the Falklands, and leading to the breakdown of my marriage

8) The Falkland Islands Police and Cable & Wireless had protected the identity of somebody who had threatened to kill me

9) Councillor Birmingham had stated in Executive Council that I should be refused the right to live and work in the Falklands because I had told the International Penguin Conference about the decline in Falklands penguins

10) Members of Executive Council had asked the Attorney General if there was any legal way of getting rid of me. After being told no they had decided to use illegal means

11) The Chief Executive, Michael Blanch, had suggested holding off their attack against me until reporters had completed their investigations to prevent their actions from being reported in the press

12) The Governor had finally refused my right to remain in the Falklands on the grounds that I had *"repeatedly sought to discredit and bring into disrepute the state of the Falkland Islands environment and the role of the Government in its protection"*.

The Chief Justice weighed up all the evidence presented, and on 25th November 2003 he gave his verdict. The verdict of the Supreme Court was that the Governor, Attorney General, Chief Executive, and the elected members of Executive Council had behaved in an illegal manner for improper motives, and that their actions were *"morally and constitutionally indefensible"*.

Chief Justice Wood stated in his summing up: *"It is not in dispute that the Applicant has published a number of articles highly critical of the Government and its policies. There have been produced to me a number of extracts of the minutes of Executive Council and of papers produced by the Government Secretariat for consideration by the Executive Council all in connection with this application.*

"In a report dated 15th October 2002, the Principal Immigration Officer (Pete King) recommended to the Executive Council of 24th October 2002 that the application be refused, and added his own comment to the effect that he too was "concerned about the damage the applicant appears to be trying to inflict on the Falkland Islands Government, and the consequent impact it is likely to have on the Islands' reputation on the world stage". The report concluded with a number of observations regarding the possible consequence of refusal.

"I have gone on to consider a further report of the Principal Immigration Officer dated 28th November 2002. The minutes disclose what in my view is a particularly significant debate which took place. On that occasion, one member enquired as to whether "there was any legal way that the application for status by the Applicant could be refused". I note that, with what proved to be significant prescience the Attorney General observed that "the essential problem is that Mr Bingham will claim that he has been victimised because the Falkland Islands Government do not like what he is saying and that is a breach of his fundamental rights to freedom of speech". It is apparent by this time that other members of Executive Council were concerned regarding the possibility of legal proceedings and indeed one enquired as to whether or not minutes of Executive Council meetings might have to be disclosed.

"Finally the Governor recalls "I was not personally persuaded that they were relevant and appropriate grounds on which to refuse the application. I voiced my concerns in this respect to the Attorney General. I

was advised that my letter should include them - I was told that it should accurately reflect the advice that I received at the meeting from Executive Council".

"The Governor goes on to say that he made it known to members of Executive Council his marked dissatisfaction with the grounds upon which to refuse the application but that he considered himself constrained to include in any decision the reasons and recommendation of Executive Council in communicating his decision to Mr Bingham.

"I begin by addressing the issue as to the identity of the person or body in whom the decision is vested by the legislation set out above. I conclude that it is vested in the Governor, and the Governor alone, in consultation with Executive Council. There is, quite simply, no provision in the Constitution requiring the Governor to act on the advice of Executive Council. That he wrongly fettered the exercise of his discretion in such a manner would have led me to find that the decision was flawed for procedural impropriety, even had I not found the decision to be flawed on substantive grounds.

"I am drawn inescapably to the conclusion that the decision to refuse the application was permeated inextricably by constitutionally improper motive. Executive Council had formed the view that by reason of his criticism of the Government and of its policies and by reason of what might be termed his "anti-establishment" views, the Applicant did not deserve Falkland Islands status, and the only remaining issue was how the refusal consequent upon such a view might be justified.

"Section 10 of the Constitution guarantees freedom of expression, including the freedom to hold opinions without interference. This is a powerful and fundamental freedom underpinning democratic society. It is not qualified by allowing the expression of only those views which are acceptable to the Government or to any particular part of society. A freedom to praise Government but not to oppose it is a chimera; it is not a freedom at all. This is not what the Falkland Islands constitution is about. That principle was not adhered to in this particular instance.

"I have concluded that the hostility engendered by the Applicant's views underlay the whole of the decision making process within Executive Council. In reaching this conclusion I have had careful and detailed regard to the minutes and papers of Executive Council as disclosed in these proceedings. Executive Council does not emerge from this case with any credit. The fact that Mr Bingham has been penalised for his views is constitutionally and morally indefensible.

"James Wood, Chief Justice of the Supreme Court, 25th November 2003"

The Falklands people had won a major victory in the fight for democracy, and even the local newspaper was jubilant. *"Bingham wins in Supreme Court"* and *"Morally and Constitutionally Indefensible"* were the headlines reporting the condemnation of the Governor and Executive Council. The Supreme Court had laid the blame on both. Executive Council were charged with behaving illegally in pursuit of what the Chief Justice had described as "improper motives", whilst the Governor was held accountable through weakness and indecision. He had failed to take control of the situation, and had failed to stop a process of discrimination which he knew to be illegal and immoral.

Now that the facts were out in the open, Falkland Islands residents were outraged, and demanded the resignation of the Governor and his corrupt officials. The newspaper was full of letters demanding a public apology from government, and an explanation as to how such corruption could have been allowed to occur unhindered at the very highest level of government. The radio station held a phone in, and during public meetings between the public and Councillors, the public continually demanded the resignation of those responsible.

But this was the Falklands. The Governor and Executive Council knew that in reality there was little that either the public or the law could do about the situation. They were the Falklands Regime. They were above the law. The Falklands Regime made their own laws, and despite being a democracy in name, and a British Overseas Territory, neither the Falklands people nor the British government had any real say in what went on.

As a result of my case the Falkland Islands Government had already introduced new laws preventing government employees from criticising the Falkland Islands Government. With over half the population obliged to remain silent, it was easy for the government to hold their ground and sit out the unrest. This was Falklands democracy, and the power to remove corrupt politicians within the Falklands Regime had been subtly controlled, all in the public interest of course.

And as for the justice system, the Falklands was a long way from Britain, the only authority which even had the pretence of issuing justice. The Falkland Islands Government knew that they could just ignore the Supreme Court ruling, and as an independent nation nobody could touch them - just as Falklands Conservation had ignored their condemnation by the Charity Commission, just as the Falkland Islands Police had been beyond the reach of Interpol and the Police Complaints Authority. As always the Falklands Regime was only answerable to itself, and that's the way they liked it.

Councillor Mike Summers told a Public Meeting that they were not going to allow me to continue my work on penguins just because "some judge" said so. That "some judge" to which Mike Summers referred, was the Chief Justice of the Supreme Court. Under Falklands law, and under the laws governing the Falklands' status as a British Overseas Territory, the Supreme Court represented the very highest level of authority. It represented the British Crown and British Justice, demanding total obedience and respect from those who swore allegiance. That Councillor Summers could dismiss the Supreme Court ruling publicly in such a disrespectful manner, showed just how much above the law the Falklands Regime considered themselves to be. The Falkland Islands Government's public remarks about the Chief Justice and the Supreme Court showed contempt not only for the law, but also for the British Crown and the British people.

The Editor of Penguin News, Jenny Cockwell, wrote an editorial which said *"Chief Justice Woods found Executive Council's decision 'morally and constitutionally indefensible'. That's a pretty strong sentiment. So will we see hands held up and an admission of 'Sorry we made a mistake'? It doesn't look like it. The statement issued by Executive Council this week in response to Chief Justice Wood's judgement didn't include the merest hint of an apology. The statement could have been the perfect opportunity to publicly take on board the Chief Justice's words and apologise to Mr Bingham for this gross breach of his constitutional rights, and to the public as a whole for this error. After all the judgement has come from the Supreme Court - the most authoritative court in the land.*" (Penguin News 28th November 2003)

The following week she wrote "*The public's angry response to the lack of apology from councillors following the Bingham judgement is clearly reflected in this week's letter page and by the number of calls we've had to the office over the past few days.*" (Penguin News 5th December 2003)

The Penguin News was full of letters of support for me, condemning the Falkland Islands Government for their treatment of me and their failure to apologise. The letters included the following statements:

- "*The total disregard by Councillors for Mr Bingham's constitutional rights is what should be at the front of all our minds when we call upon our Councillors to justify their actions. They have acted, and continue to do so by their unwillingness to apologise, in a manner more akin to some tin-pot dictatorship than a community that likes to think of itself as democratic. If this community really wants to be democratic, and perhaps more importantly to be seen to be democratic, then we must demand that the relevant Councillors explain their actions publicly. Many people died liberating these islands so that we might be free. That freedom was hard won, don't let politicians take it away without a fight. Today it was Mike Bingham, tomorrow it might be you or your children."* (Penguin News 5th December 2003)

- *"Councillor Summers is completely wrong when he says that the Bingham case was about the right to choose who becomes a citizen. The case did not concern the right of government to make choices. The case actually concerned the need for government to act within the law when exercising its powers, not to impose personal prejudice on its choices, and not to abuse its authority. In acting as it did, Executive Council abused the trust we as citizens put in Government to act fairly, impartially and properly."* (Penguin News 12th December 2003)

- *"In response to the penguin deaths, we tried to tell Falklands Conservation but no one bothered to come out to look. The problem started in April 2002 when we lost 500 gentoos and 2000 rockhoppers. Falklands Conservation wouldn't come out, so we called Mike Bingham who did come out."* (Penguin News 20th December 2003)

- *"I accuse certain members of this administration of the unjust treatment handed out to Mike Bingham. In fact it is against the Haig Convention of Human Rights which this administration has signed up to. I understand the reason Mr Bingham is being treated so is that he had the audacity to question imaginative accountancy by Falklands Conservation regarding penguin numbers. I, like Falklands Conservation, am not an expert on penguins, but what does it take for these people to realise that there is a problem? Emaciated penguins outside the Falklands Conservation office with a begging bowl, squawking up 'Please can we have some more'? For evil to triumph requires only that good men do nothing."* (Penguin News 20th December 2003)

- *"Could the Attorney General tell us if he was aware that the decision by Executive Council to refuse Mike Bingham's application on the grounds that he was critical of government was a breach of his Constitutional rights to freedom of speech. If he was aware of this, could he please tell us what action he took to defend Mr Bingham's Constitutional Rights?"* (Penguin News 12th December 2003). We know from the minutes of the 28th November 2002 Executive Council Meeting that the Attorney General, David Lang, had already instructed Executive Council that their actions would be illegal under the Constitutional rights to freedom of speech. Executive Council not only decided to ignore the law, but the Attorney General himself had been part of the Executive Council which had done so.

On the international arena the Falkland Islands Government were exposed and humiliated. Despite attempts by the British and Falklands governments to prevent the British press running the story, the story did hit the headlines, from London to Buenos Aires. The Falklands was exposed as an outpost of political greed and corruption, where politicians lined their pockets with money from commercial fishing, whilst penguins starved. Gone was the pedestal of moral superiority from which the Falklands had looked down on their South American neighbours for so many years. It had now been officially declared by the Supreme Court that the Falkland Islands Government were corrupt, committing human rights violations in an attempt to cover up the damage which commercial fishing was causing to penguin populations.

Because I had won my case, the Supreme Court had ordered the Falkland Islands Government to pay all my legal fees, on top of their own legal fees and court costs. In all the Supreme Court hearing cost the Falkland Islands tax-payers over £65,000 (US$100,000). I did not have to pay a single penny.

I was flooded by letters of support. The Falklands newspapers carried letters of support from members of the public, but that was nothing to the flood of emails and letters I received from people all over the world congratulating me on my defence of Falklands penguins, and my stand against human rights violations in the Falklands. I was offered money for my story from journalists, and sent money to continue saving penguins. I was also included in the highly prestigious publication "Who's Who", in recognition of my work to save penguins in the Falkland Islands.

Despite this, Councillor Mike Summers had made it quite clear at the Public Meeting that the Falklands Regime was not going to let 'some judge' alter their plans to stop my work in the Falklands, one way or another. Such arrogance and contempt towards the Chief Justice and the Supreme Court left me in no doubt that to return to the Falklands would put me at great personal risk. The people exposed for corruption wanted revenge, and since the Supreme Court ruling had not stopped them, it was hard to imagine what would. Sooner or later my luck was bound to run out, and they would succeed in framing me for something serious in such a way that I would not be able to prove my innocence.

By contrast the British, Chilean and Argentine governments were all supporting me to monitor and protect penguins in Chile and Argentina. Indeed the British government had offered me over £30,000 (US$45,000) to set up a long-term penguin monitoring programme in South America. Faced with eventual imprisonment at the hands of corrupt government officials in the Falklands, or working with the support of three governments in South America, the choice was easy.

By now I was weary of looking over my shoulder, of continually checking my house in search of false evidence that the Falklands police might have planted, of being unable to start a family for fear of the harassment they would suffer for my beliefs. Working in Chile and Argentina was such a joy. Both countries held a genuine concern for the protection of wildlife, not a desire to set up a phoney front to give the impression of doing something, as was happening in the Falklands. This was evident from the responses to outside monitoring.

Whilst the Falklands Regime tried to frame, deport and even threaten to kill anybody who conducted independent research into their handling of the environment, the governments of Chile and Argentina openly welcomed independent scrutiny. Their conservation efforts were genuine. They had nothing to hide, and hoped to benefit from outside scrutiny that could improve the work they were doing.

The Falkland Islands Government, aided and abetted by Falklands Conservation, were only interested in setting up worthless conservation initiatives to give the impression of doing something, whilst refusing to introduce any real protection that might impact on revenue from commercial fishing and oil exploration. This was why they did not want independent scrutiny. They did not want reports and advise from the world's penguin experts, nor World Heritage status from Birdlife International, nor a meddling do-gooder looking over their shoulder.

I had spent 11 years in the Falklands. Virtually everybody who lived in the Falklands knew the state of play. They knew that the immense wealth coming into the Falklands through commercial fishing was at the expense of penguins and other wildlife. Individual opinions only differed in so far as which was the most important - money or penguins. Thrown into this equation was the continuing dispute with Argentina, and the sad fact that financial wealth from commercial fishing helped to finance this dispute. To many it was a choice between penguins and political independence.

It would take a lifetime to change such attitudes, and I doubted that I would survive another 6 months in the Falklands before being framed and thrown into prison, or worse, an accident or a mysterious disappearance. Such things had happened before. A British soldier called Private Addis had disappeared without trace in the Falklands, and the only witness had been killed in a house fire just a few hours later. For somebody to die in a house fire within 24 hours of witnessing a murder, could only be seen as suspicious, and yet the Falkland Islands Police had declared it an accident.

I knew that if I were to die in a similar 'accident', that the Falkland Islands Police would protect my killer in the same way as they had protected the person who had threatened to kill me - freedom from prosecution and concealment of his identity - all in the public interest, of course.

In prison, or buried in some unknown peat bog like poor Addis, I would have been no use to the penguins. But in South America, with the support of three governments, I had the opportunity to make a real contribution to penguin protection. Following a series of meetings with government officials, a long-term strategy for monitoring and protecting penguins was agreed, and the Organizacion para la Conservacion de los Pingüinos was born.

I had already been offered permanent residency status for both Chile and Argentina, so I found an apartment in Rio Gallegos, and returned to the Falklands on 14th February 2004 to pack my belongings to ship across to my new home in Argentina. Whilst packing my belongings I found a bag containing dozens of small sachets of white powder, which could only have been drugs. I flushed them down the toilet, and took heart from the fact that my decision to leave the Falklands was the right one.

Everything that I did not ship across to Argentina I took to the public tip and burned, so that nothing could be used to incriminate me. The police raid that I expected over the planted drugs never took place, either because they had been planted to discredit me prior to the court case, or because knowing that I was now leaving the Falklands, the Falklands Regime no longer felt it necessary to try and frame me again.

I finally left the Falklands on 28th February 2004, and felt a great weight lifted off my shoulders. My Falklands house, which I had spent so long building single-handed, was sold, and I bought a new house in Rio Gallegos, just 100 metres from the Argentine President's house.

I regretted that I was abandoning my work in the Falklands. I regretted leaving the many good people who had lifted me on a wave of public support following my court victory. But I knew in my heart that my work to protect penguins would be of much greater value working in an honest country. I also wanted to think of my own future. I did not want to spend my whole life alone. No longer under constant police harassment and death threats, I wanted some day to find a new lady friend with whom to share my life, without fear of putting her in harm's way.

I have no doubt that there are many places in the world where much greater acts of corruption take place, where government officials are at liberty to murder opponents without fear of arrest. But when one bears in mind that the Falklands population is only 2,500 inhabitants, I doubt that anywhere on earth is government corruption more permeated into the very fabric of society. Through the police, customs and immigration, to the radio station, newspaper, hospital and post office, the Falklands Regime can manipulate and harass almost any aspect of private life if they are so motivated. Add to that the belief within the highest levels of government that they are above the law, and you have a government that is rotten to the core.

That such a corrupt regime operates under the protection of the British government is an insult to every hard working Briton. British servicemen gave their lives in 1982, under the false belief that they were upholding democracy. These servicemen made that sacrifice to ensure that the people of the Falklands would have the right to lead their lives free from political tyranny; free to hold beliefs and opinions without oppression.

It is ironic that 22 years after British troops died for democracy in the Falklands, that a British citizen would be forced to flee the Falklands to escape political corruption and death threats, to seek democracy and freedom of speech in Argentina.

FALKLANDS WEALTH

No virtuous beauty can life bestow,
on men who great starvation know.
But those of wealth should see things true,
that life is more than me and you.

As penguins fish and eagles fly,
does life's mystique not catch your eye?
Without their spectre to behold,
what purpose be to all grow old?

Should cars and TV take the place,
of all we lose of nature's grace?
To crave more wealth than we can spend,
we risk a world we cannot mend.

When oil and penguins both are through,
and children ask us what we do.
Perhaps recall what once we had,
and why we thought is was so bad.

Mike Bingham (May 1996)

ABOUT THE AUTHOR

Mike Bingham has worked for the United States Government, British Government, Chilean Government and Argentine Government helping to preserve endangered wildlife. In 1993 Bingham was appointed Conservation Officer for the Falkland Islands, embroiling him in a savage struggle with greedy government officials, who would stop at nothing to protect financial interests in commercial fishing and oil exploration.

When Bingham's penguin research revealed massive population declines resulting from over-fishing, he was offered a large pay rise to cover up his findings. When he refused, he was kicked out as Conservation Officer, and forced to continue his research with his own savings. But Bingham's work was of such high standard that it attracted the financial backing of the British, Chilean and Argentine governments, and the Falklands' first independent conservation organisation was born.

When oil exploration began in the Falklands, Mike Bingham led a protest against the hundreds of penguins that were dying from oil pollution. Government officials decided that Bingham posed a threat to their future wealth, and began a hideous campaign to remove him.

Discovering firearms planted under his bed just prior to a police raid, was the first of many lucky escapes for Bingham, as various attempts to frame, deport, and kill him failed. When this corruption was eventually exposed in the world press, Bingham found his family the target of a vicious retaliation that forced them to flee the Falklands. Bingham took the Falkland Islands Government to the Supreme Court, which ruled that the Governor, Attorney General, Chief Executive and Executive Council had committed acts of human rights abuse that were "morally and constitutionally indefensible".

Struggling against a backdrop of personal tragedy and illness, Bingham brought the starvation of 5 million penguins, high-level government corruption, and the abuse of human rights, to the attention of the outside world, but at considerable personal cost. When the Falkland Islands Government announced to the public that they were not going to be stopped by the Supreme Court ruling, Bingham was forced to seek safety in Argentina.

It is ironic that twenty years after British troops died for democracy in the Falklands War, a British citizen would be forced to flee the Falklands to escape political corruption and death threats, to seek democracy and freedom of speech in Argentina.

CPSIA information can be obtained at www.ICGtesting.com
Printed in the USA
BVOW021802171111

276379BV00001B/1/A